FROM BLACKLAND PRAIRIE TO BLACKTOP

A History of Collin County

By Randolph W. Farmer

A publication of the North Texas History Center

Historical Publishing Network
A division of Lammert Incorporated
San Antonio, Texas

Bushy bluestem grasses preserved at the Connemara Conservancy show the native lands of North Texas. Little bluestem and big bluestem grasses grew in abundance on the prairies of North Texas. These thick grasses created incredible obstacles to the pioneers.

PHOTOGRAPH COURTESY OF MICHELLE SCHNEIDER.

First Edition

ISBN: 9781935377443

Library of Congress Card Catalog Number: 2011927590

From Blackland Prairie to Blacktop: A History of Collin County

author: Randolph W. Farmer

contributing writer for sharing the heritage: Eric Dabney

Historical Publishing Network

president: Ron Lammert

project manager: Sydney McNew

administration: Donna M. Mata, Melissa G. Quinn

book sales: Dee Steidle

production: Colin Hart, Evelyn Hart, Glenda Tarazon Krouse, Omar Wright

CONTENTS

CHAPTER I

THE FIRST INHABITANTS IN COLLIN COUNTY

✧

The landscape of North Texas prior to settlement by the most recent round of immigrants.

PHOTOGRAPH COURTESY OF MICHELLE SCHNEIDER.

Modern-day Collin County consists of 851 square miles in Northeast Texas drained by two separate branches of the Trinity River: the Elm Fork on the eastern side, and the East Fork on the western side. Except for a small section of the western part of the county, almost all of it lies upon the Blackland Prairie, a true tall grass prairie that extends over 12.6 million acres. With over 570 species, subspecies, and varieties of grasses, Texas leads the nation in dispersion of this form of plant life. Although less than one percent of the original Blackland Prairie remains as it once was 15,000 years ago, there was grass—and lots of it. This naturally attracted the animals that fed upon it.

From 30,000 to 22,500 B.C. most of the currently forested regions of the Central United States were covered by a vast prairie. An Ice Age began around 22,500 B.C. with glaciers reaching their maximum growth about 20,000 years ago. What human beings there were on the northern prairie would have been pushed farther south as the leading southern edge of the glaciers stopped around the area of current-day St. Louis, Missouri and Kansas. At this time the average annual temperature in Texas was about nine degrees cooler than today, which may sound insignificant unless one has spent a winter night on the open prairies of North Texas. In today's Collin County, average temperatures range from a high of 96°F to a low of 34°F.

Evidence of human habitation in the Collin County area reliably dates from 11,600 years ago. Approximately fourteen miles west of the Collin/Denton County border are two of the oldest late-Pleistocene archeological sites in North America, near the little town of Aubrey. Discovered in 1988 in the flood plain of the Elm Fork of the Trinity River, the Aubrey site has to date yielded the oldest reliable radiocarbon dating of the presence of the Clovis culture. It is highly likely that these Clovis people followed the course of the river and its tributaries into Collin County on occasion. These early humans knew no boundaries, and their distinctive artifacts are found from Alaska to south Texas. The origins of the Clovis people are a mystery, as they were a nomadic culture that left a light footprint on their environment.

The Aubrey site so close to Collin County has yielded much information that contradicts widely held beliefs of the nature of Clovis culture. The site contains two distinct camps with differing functional purpose, one exclusively for the butchering of animals. The numerous burned remains of animals found in their hearth areas show a diet and an enterprise more varied than previously thought. The Clovis people were not exclusively hunting megafauna as remains of fish, turtles, alligators, snakes, birds, rabbits, squirrel, prairie dog, rat, dire wolf, horse, white-tailed deer as well as mammoth and bison are all present. From the over 4,000 elements found in their fires it has been discovered that their diet was dominated by much smaller animals: turtles, rabbits, wood rats and deer. The butchering camp was mainly used for dressing bison and the occasional mammoth, which suggests specialization, flexibility and division of labor. Clovis people were more adaptable to their surroundings and resource base than considered possible for such a highly mobile society. Yet the evidence does point to a temporary or perhaps seasonal occupation of the sites on an infrequent basis.

About twenty miles south of Aubrey on the Elm Fork of the Trinity River is the Lewisville Clovis site, originally radiocarbon dated at 37,000+ years old when found in 1957. Now under the waters of Lake Lewisville, the site was re-evaluated by scientists under the direction of persons associated with the Smithsonian Institution during a period of prolonged drought that re-exposed the site. This newer data suggest a likely habitation some 12,000 years ago, making it one of the Western Hemisphere's oldest verifiable cultural sites. The exact date cannot be determined with total confidence due to the fact that these Clovis people used lignite to augment the 21 fire hearths found there. Within the hearths were the burned bones of mammoths, horses, camels, bison, bears, and other types of animals. Lignite, a form of low-grade coal, is found in some of the Cretaceous-age seams of rock strata throughout Texas. The Cretaceous age dates back some 65 million years to the time when today's Blackland Prairie was at the bottom of the ocean; that, and the carbon-based nature of lignite, contaminates the site for radiocarbon dating purposes. The use of lignite for fuel by the Clovis people again demonstrates their resourcefulness: they were miners and probably traders as well as hunters and butchers. The Lewisville site is once again completely under water and all the materials found in the last excavation are now in the possession of the Smithsonian Institution.

On a tributary of the Elm Fork remains of an elderly woman thought to date to the Clovis period have been found. Sand that the body was buried in dates to the Pleistocene era. The fact that the woman was found relatively intact indicates that she was given a burial and was not alone when she died. She was buried six feet under the surface of Denton County so that her body would not be scavenged by animals or washed downstream by the waters of what is now called Denton Creek. Although the Clovis people demonstrated adaptability, resourcefulness and social cohesion, they were still traveling in isolated bands and did not settle for long in any location. By 8,000 B.C. the massive glaciers of the Ice Age had receded from the prairie, and Clovis Man seems to have disappeared. Some believe that the culture died out with the disappearance of the megafauna—the mammoths, bison, horses and camels now extinct in North America—but the Clovis sites near Collin County provide evidence of a much more varied diet than that. Others believe that Clovis culture was wiped from the face of the earth by the explosion of a comet in

Above and below: Treasures of The Caddo People.

Distribution of Late Prehistoric Sites along the East Fork and Trinity River Watershed

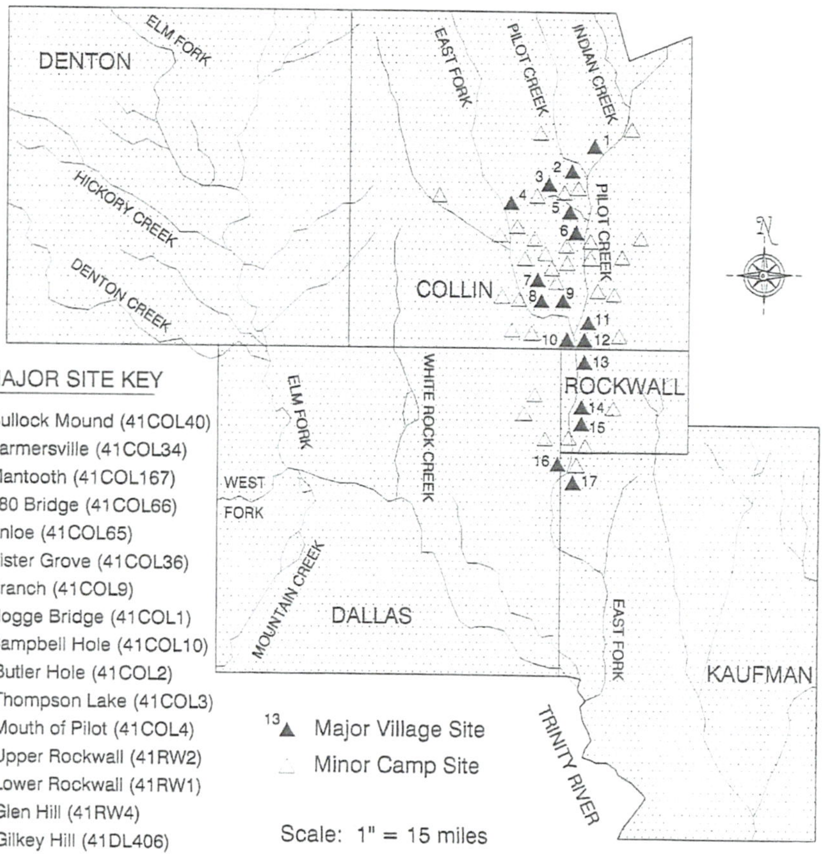

MAJOR SITE KEY

1. Bullock Mound (41COL40)
2. Farmersville (41COL34)
3. Mantooth (41COL167)
4. 380 Bridge (41COL66)
5. Enloe (41COL65)
6. Sister Grove (41COL36)
7. Branch (41COL9)
8. Hogge Bridge (41COL1)
9. Campbell Hole (41COL10)
10. Butler Hole (41COL2)
11. Thompson Lake (41COL3)
12. Mouth of Pilot (41COL4)
13. Upper Rockwall (41RW2)
14. Lower Rockwall (41RW1)
15. Glen Hill (41RW4)
16. Gilkey Hill (41DL406)
17. Ragland (41KF4)

✧

The East Fork and Trinity River watershed archeological site survey, 1973-1975.

MAP COURTESY OF THE HEARD MUSEUM OF NATURAL SCIENCE.

Earth's atmosphere, changing the environment drastically and suddenly. It is also possible that Clovis people intermarried with other cultures and were simply assimilated. The Clovis culture lasted for about 500 years; others took their place on the Blackland Prairie.

Archeological evidence seems to indicate a shift in habitation to either the east or west of Collin County after the disappearance of the Clovis people. There were hunters in East Texas around 8,000 B.C. and they likely would have occasion to chase game on the Blackland Prairie while preferring to live among the pine trees of the great southern forest. Water holes had evaporated and the plains had dried up. The Archaic period beginning about 6,000 B.C. was one of vacillating climatic conditions followed by a warmer period from 5,000 to 3,000 B.C. Around 3,800 B.C. the Proto-Iroquoian-Caddoan community in the Eastern United States had broken apart, and by 2,000 B.C. the Proto-Caddoan groups began to migrate up the tributaries of the Mississippi River, drawn by an increase in moisture and game on the Blackland Prairie. Until about 2,500 B.C. the record indicates Texas was sparsely populated by small, nomadic bands; after that there is a marked population increase. Recent expansion of the President George Bush Turnpike has uncovered a Late Archaic Period (1500 B.C. to 700 A.D.) site near Rowlett Creek, which rises four miles west of McKinney in Collin County and until recent times fed into the East Fork of the Trinity River in Rockwall County. Among the deer and bison bones were found substantial trade goods and materials obtained from other cultures far away. This newly uncovered site is still being evaluated and apparently was inhabited through the Late Prehistoric period from 700 A.D. to 1600 A.D. These people were most likely the ancestors of the Native American or Indian tribes found after the Pre-Columbian period, but it was not until after 500 B.C. that these "proto-Indians" began to settle in established villages. Most of their permanent settlements were in East Texas, and the people that built them are known to us today as "the Woodland people", the ancestral culture of the Iroquois and Caddo. It is with their appearance that domestication of animals and plants, including corn, appears to have taken hold in East Texas.

When corn culture finally established itself in Texas around 700 A.D., the seed was planted for what became known as the Caddo Indian culture. They were the westernmost members of the Mississippian Cultural Tradition and eventually their descendants would expand into Collin County. In eastern Collin County, in an area now under the waters of Lake Lavon, is the Hogge Bridge archaeological site, explored in 1950 after no less than 25 prehistoric sites were found in the area. Pottery associated with the Caddo Indians of East Texas was found in one site, which dates from the Prehistoric

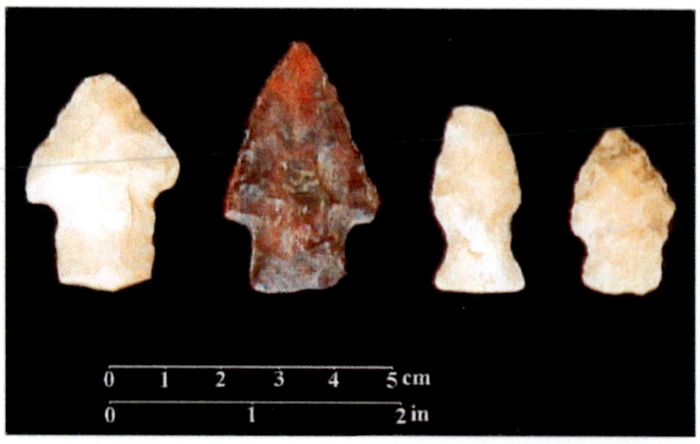

(Pre-Columbian) period. The largest Caddo tribe, the Hasinai, have a version of their creation story that has survived to this day:

> In the earliest times, darkness ruled over the land. In this darkness only one man lived as a Hasinai. Around him, a village emerged. As its occupants grew in number, they noticed that the man seemed to be everywhere. Then he disappeared, returning with all types of food in the form of seeds. The unknown man called the people together and patiently explained that the seeds were food for Hasinai use. He then gave the seeds to each of the people present. On one memorable occasion, the tammas (town criers) were sent out to tell the Hasinai that the caddi (chiefs) wanted them to assemble....
>
> The people formed themselves into groups and selected a leader known as a canaha, or community headman, for each group. The caddi called these leaders together and gave each one a drum. He explained to the canahas that they must sing and beat their drums as the people moved from the world in darkness to the new world....the people began moving to the west, emerging in groups in a new world of light....When the first people emerged into the new world, the men, aside from the leaders, carried pipes and pieces of flint. The women carried the seed corn and pumpkin seeds that had been given them in the old world.[1]

Maize agriculture resulted in a population boom for the Caddo, who soon formed different tribes based on kinship. By 900 A.D. the Caddo had developed a complex society and religion. They lived in beehive shaped homes made of grass and cane in small communities widely dispersed across Northeast Texas, including Collin County. These houses varied in size according to social status, but generally were forty or fifty feet high and sixty feet wide. Along the interior walls were beds attached above the ground; the floors were swept clean and covered with finely made mats and rugs. Three or four families would occupy one house.

Caddo ceramics are among the most highly prized of the prehistoric world of North America, and Caddo bows made of locally available bois d'arc wood were traded to other tribes further west for goods such as volcanic glass (obsidian) and turquoise. The small Caddo villages were scattered around a larger ceremonial complex consisting of earthen mounds used for religious and civic ceremonies. Many of these mounds lie north of Collin County along the Red River. One such mound complex can be seen today near Alto, Texas, in Cherokee County. Here they worshiped the Corn Goddess and the sun, but the supreme deity worshiped by Caddos was known as Ahahayo, literally, "Father Above" in their language. Ahahayo was the creator of all, punishing bad deeds and rewarding good ones. Communication with Ahahayo was the responsibility of the xinesi, a spiritual leader who tended a sacred fire kept perpetually burning. The eternal flame was housed in a special building inhabited by two

Left: Non-projectile points from the Frognot site. Top row, left to right: Leaf-shaped biface/knives (2), Unifacial flake scrapers (2), East Fork Gouge. Bottom row left to right: "Turtleback" side scraper, Guadalupe Biface, Chopper.

PHOTOGRAPH COURTESY OF THE DALLAS ARCHAEOLOGICAL SOCIETY.

Right: Paleoindian dart points from the Frognot site, approximately five miles northeast of Farmersville. Top row, left to right: San Patrice (2), Dalton, Midland, Plainview. Bottom row, left to right: Angostura, Scottsbluff.

PHOTOGRAPH COURTESY OF THE DALLAS ARCHAEOLOGICAL SOCIETY.

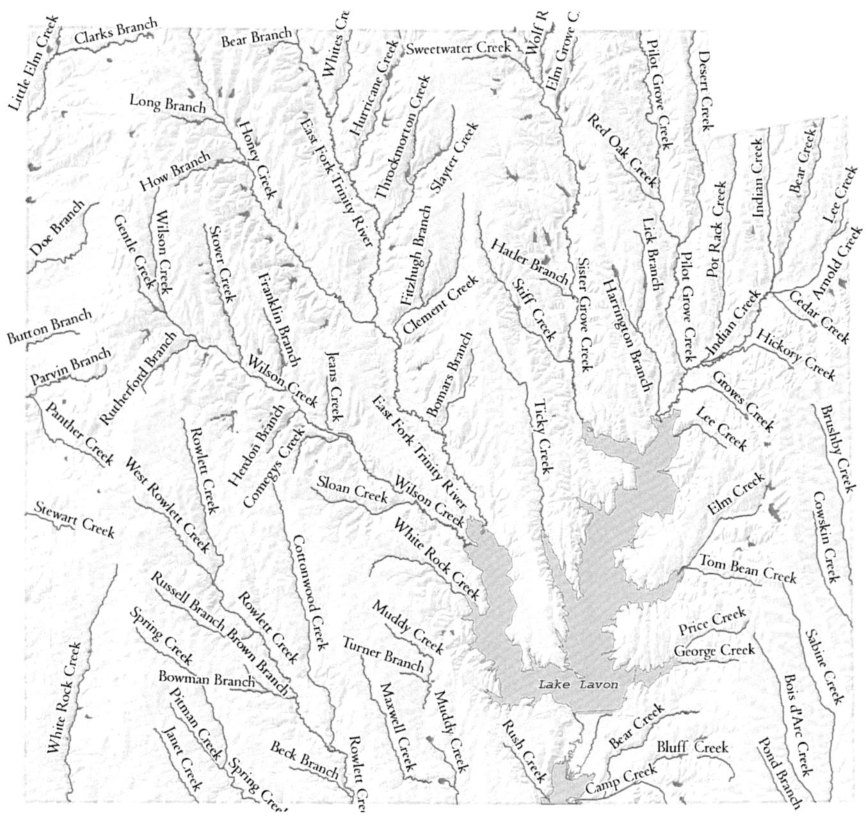

✧

Above: Watershed map of Collin County.

MAP COURTESY OF BRET FENSTER, GIS SERVICES, COLLIN COUNTY.

Below: Map of counties of North Central Texas.

MAP COURTESY OF BRET FENSTER, GIS SERVICES, COLLIN COUNTY.

divine children, known as the coninisi. Only the xinesi could see and speak with the coninisi, who communicated the will of Ahahayo to the tribe's spiritual leader. In this ceremonial arrangement are the echoes of the Proto-Iroquoian-Caddoan culture, for the Iroquois are known to have believed in divine twins, one who personified evil and one of good character.

By 1200 A.D. maize agriculture intensified further as the Caddo perfected their growing techniques, able to harvest two different varieties per year, as well as pumpkin, squash, beans, and other plants. By 1300 all of the tribes were consuming large amounts of maize; by the year 1500 the population reached its all-time peak, estimated at 200,000, stretching from the Trinity River to the Arkansas River. This sizable population would soon fall prey to a previously unseen evil: European-borne disease. As the Caddos maintained substantial trade with many of the Indian tribes in Texas, they came in contact with tribes exposed to the four survivors of the Narvaez Expedition, one of whom was the now famous Cabeza de Vaca. The four Europeans had been shipwrecked on the Texas coast in 1528 and spent seven years wandering the countryside, exposing tribes to unknown diseases to which they had no immunity. Soon enough the Caddo were directly exposed to European contagion by the arrival in their territory of survivors of the Hernando De Soto Mississippi River expedition of 1542. De Soto had died but his successor, Luis de Moscoso described meeting people he called the Naguatex. The term Naguatex is a corruption of two Caddoan words: nawi and techas, which mean "friends down there." Moscoso and his men wandered the Blackland Prairie, traveling a course parallel to the Red River, a relatively short distance from northern Collin County. At least one man from these two Spanish expeditions may have wandered through Collin County; a chain-mail gauntlet, a halberd and a horseman's spur were found together on the Trinity River in Dallas County. The Kichai tribe of that county spoke a Caddoan language and was a close trading partner with the Caddo, so it is a near certainty that the Caddo of Collin County were exposed at an early date to European disease.

By the time Europeans reappeared in Caddo country in the late 1600s, the tribes' population had been reduced by 95 percent, decimated by catastrophic epidemics of disease. One positive aspect of contact with Europeans, especially the French, was the acquisition of horses. The Caddo put these horses to good use in their annual winter buffalo hunts; their success as a people had always depended on their ability to acquire food. The early Europeans that encountered the Caddo people were impressed with their robust physiques and fine features, noting that their faces were thinner than other tribes

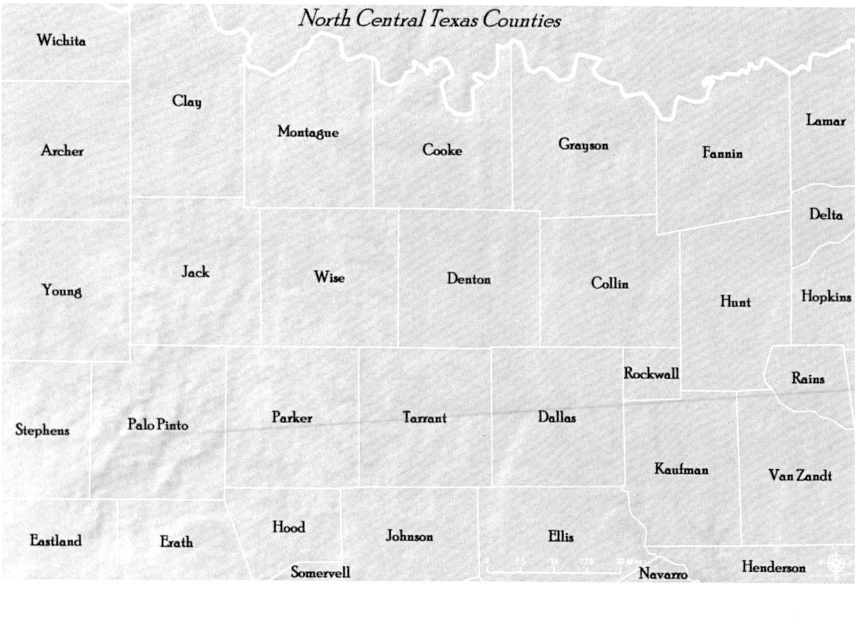

A Caddo village.

they had met. The French also provided the Caddo with European weapons technology, which allowed them greater prominence among neighboring tribes. By 1750 they had the latest weapons and soon began to trade them with their allies, the Comanche and Wichita tribes, who like they, were at war with the encroaching Apache Indians. Under Spanish rule from 1767 until 1803, the Caddo entered a period of decline, but rebounded when the United States acquired the Louisiana Territory, stimulating trade in East Texas. However by 1825 the Caddo were being displaced from East Texas by the Cherokee Indians who had been driven from their homes east of the Mississippi River. Complicating things further, the emergence of the Independent Republic of Texas in 1836 proved to be disastrous for the Caddo.

The Caddo were caught in a web of intrigue spun upon them by agents of the governments of Mexico, the United States, and the Republic of Texas, all of whom had designs upon the land that once belonged to the Caddo. Scattered incidents of violence between Caddo and Anglo settlers began to increase. The Cherokee were used as pawns against the Caddo, who were coerced into signing a treaty with the Texan government on August 21, 1837. Traders began to ply them with alcohol and the Caddo were cheated out of their annuity payments guaranteed by treaty by Indian agents assigned to protect their interests. After this happened two years in a row, a number of Caddo abandoned all hope and began to raid white settlers, attacking a party of 18 Texas Rangers on November 10, 1837, near the headwaters of the Trinity River and killing 10 of them. The survivors staggered into a Caddo village located near the forks of the Trinity River, where they found all of the male inhabitants heavily armed with rifles and the women with bow and arrows. Even in this difficult situation, the Caddo allowed the Rangers to stay the night and tend their wounds. Relations with the Texans had gotten off to a bad start for the Caddo, and would worsen with the election of Mirabeau Buonaparte Lamar as president of the Republic of Texas. Elected on September 3, 1838, Lamar almost immediately called for the extermination of all Indians in Texas. In this hostile atmosphere, and as more Anglo settlers moved into the area that later became Collin County, more violence was inevitable.

CHAPTER II

PIONEERS

✧

Collin McKinney's 1846 home after it was moved from Anna to Finch Park in McKinney. Several generations of school children toured the home before it burned in 1980.

By 1839 all of the Caddo tribes had been chased across the Red River and out of Texas by Republican troops, but were soon recognized as a peaceful tribe and allowed to return. During M. B. Lamar's disastrous reign as president of the fledgling Republic of Texas, the portion of the Blackland Prairie now known as Collin County did not exist, as it was still a part of Fannin County, whose county seat was established in 1840 at Warren, on the Red River. By that time the Texas Rangers began to experience some success in their battles with the nomadic Penateka Comanches, the most feared warriors of the Plains. The Penatekas were also being pressured by their northern rivals the Cheyenne and Arapaho tribes, and so in January of 1840, they made overtures of peace with the Texas government. The Texans did not understand the fragmented nature of Comanche society, and unrealistically demanded the release of all white hostages held by all factions of the Comanche nation, an act that could not be accomplished by the Penatekas, who agreed to turn over their hostages. They agreed to meet at the council house in San Antonio on March 19, 1840, when the Penatekas made good on their promise, bringing in several Mexican children and one sixteen-year old white girl, who had obviously been tortured and abused, her face disfigured.

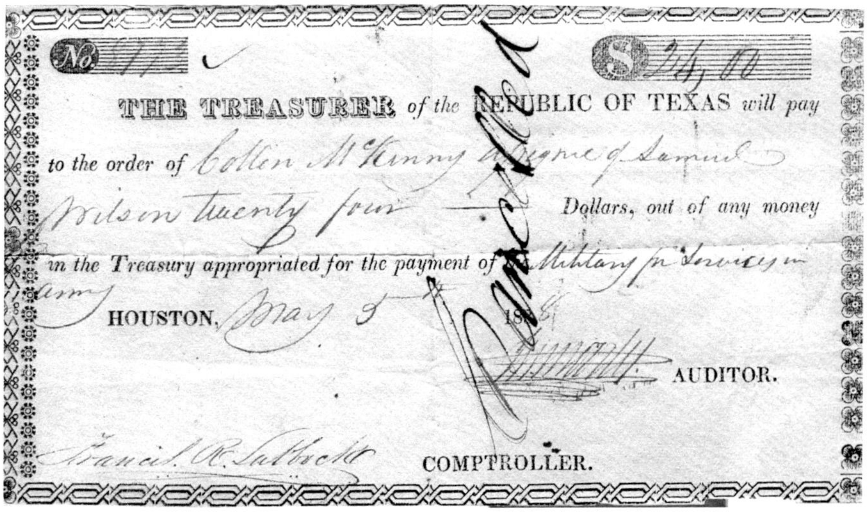

Above: A check issued to Collin McKinney from the Republic of Texas. It reads:

The Treasurer of the Republic of Texas will pay to the order of Collin McKinney_____of Samuel Wilson twenty four dollars, out of any money in the Treasury appropriated for the payment of Military for services in army.

Houston, May 5, 1838
[signed] Auditor
Francis R. Lalbock,
Comptroller

The outraged Texans then told the 33 Penateka chiefs and warriors and their entourage of 32 other Comanches in attendance that they would be held as hostages until the rest of the Anglo captives were exchanged. The Comanches panicked, and in their attempted escape all were killed except for one woman who was freed. The Council House Fight, as the incident became known, greatly enraged the Comanche tribes and their allies, who considered ambassadors of peace to be immune from acts of war; they now considered the Texans to be dishonorable and treacherous. All-out war was then inaugurated against the settlers by Comanches led by Buffalo Hump; allied tribes such as the Wichitas, Kichais and Wacos further exploited the situation.

Sam Houston was elected to a second term as president of the Republic of Texas in September, 1841 and announced the resumption of his peace policy towards the Native Americans. Before Houston could implement his policy, North Texas settlers would feel the brunt of Comanche violence. Small numbers of settlers had moved into the area beginning in 1840; McBain Jameson settled on Rowlett Creek in what is now Plano sometime after receiving a conditional land certificate on January 2, 1840. In 1841, William E. Throckmorton settled near what is now the town of Melissa. Pleasant Wilson had served as a guide for Throckmorton's party of settlers, including M. C. Clements and his sons Wesley and Buford, Jobey Fitzgerald, W. R. Garrett, Edmund Todd, Littleton Rattan and their respective families. The Clements family subsequently decided to settle closer to Fort Inglish in Fannin County, which left the rest of the party to establish the first permanent settlement in Collin County, which became known as Throckmorton's Settlement.[1]

In November 1841, Hamp Rattan, A. W. Webb and S. Silkwood were sent from the settlement to investigate the status of a supply wagon that was expected from Bird's Fort in present-day Tarrant County. On the way the three men discovered a honeybee's nest near what is now Carrollton, Texas, and were in the process of felling the tree when they were attacked by Indians. Rattan was killed instantly; the other two settlers managed to kill one Indian before escaping to Bird's Fort, where Silkwood died from exposure to the elements. On December 30, the supply wagon reached the scene of Rattan's murder and found his body guarded by his faithful dog. Hamp Rattan was just the first white settler of Collin County known to have been killed by Indians; other, more remotely located individuals may have simply "disappeared."

The following summer Throckmorton's settlement was increased by the arrival of Benjamin White, Archie White, William Pulliam, "Peg" Whistler, and John Kincaid. In November 1842, J. H. Wilcox, David Helms, and Joseph Harlan began to construct a settlement on Wilson's Creek. That same month,

Bottom, left and right: Currency of the Republic of Texas.

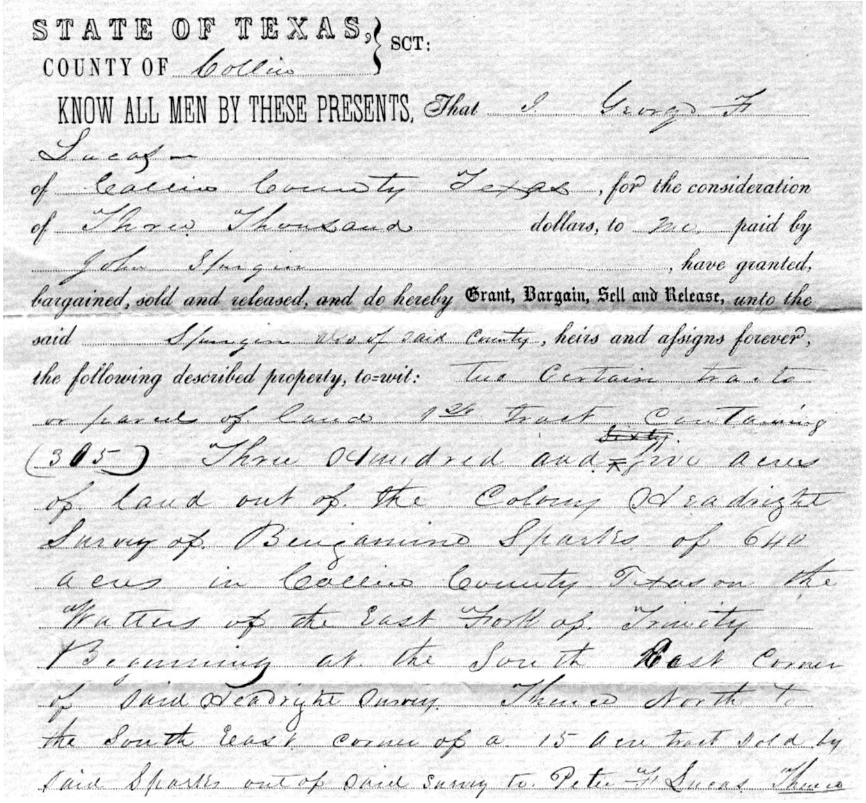
STATE OF TEXAS, } SCT:
COUNTY OF Collin

KNOW ALL MEN BY THESE PRESENTS, That I George F Lucas of Collin County Texas, for the consideration of Three Thousand dollars, to me paid by John Spurgin, have granted, bargained, sold and released, and do hereby Grant, Bargain, Sell and Release, unto the said Spurgin [illegible] of said County, heirs and assigns forever, the following described property, to-wit: Two Certain tracts or parcels of land 1st tract Containing (305) Three Hundred and sixty five acres of land out of the Colony Headright Survey of Benjamin Sparks of 640 acres in Collin County Texas on the Waters of the East Fork of Trinity Beginning at the South East Corner of said Headright Survey Thence North to the South East corner of a 15 acre tract sold by said Sparks out of said survey to Peter F Lucas Thence

✧

Land deed, State of Texas, Collin County, dated June 24, 1857, conveying land from George F. Lucas to John Spurgin. Note the phrase about halfway through the document: "...the Colony Headright survey...".

John McGarrah arrived with his family and those of Samuel Young, William Rice, and J. E. Blankenship at Throckmorton's place before relocating. About this time Wesley Clements had secured title to a new site about seven miles northwest of present-day McKinney upon which he planned to settle. Clements, Young, and Whistler then settled with their families near Honey Creek, and in December, Young went to Fort Inglish for supplies. On Christmas morning while cutting wood near their cabins, Clements and Whistler were attacked by Comanches; Whistler was killed instantly. Clements wife heard the commotion and seeing her husband fleeing toward their cabin ran out to meet him with his gun in her hands. When she reached him she found that he had already been killed and scalped. Returning to the cabin, she and Mrs. Young barred the door and held the Indians off; Mrs. Whistler had been caught outside near the stream but hid herself underwater until the Comanches left. She then ran all the way to Fort Inglish. Men from the fort later found Mrs. Young and Mrs. Clements alive; the bodies of their husbands had been horribly mutilated.

The day after the Clements-Whistler massacre, the same band of Comanches attacked the Wilson's Creek settlement. Joe Wilcox, David Helms, and Joseph Harlan managed to reach their cabin and fought off the Indians successfully. Under cover of darkness the men relocated to John McGarrah's settlement. In early 1843, Thomas J. McDonald, who had settled on Honey Creek, had his cabin ransacked by Comanches while he and his family were away visiting friends; all of his pigs and chickens were killed.[2] This same band then attacked McGarrah's settlement in February 1843, killing Dr. Calder from Dallas who was riding past on his way to Fort Inglish. The seven men at the settlement held off sixty Comanche braves with heavy rifle fire before retreating. At dark the seven men escaped to Throckmorton's settlement. A posse that attempted to overtake the raiding party was unsuccessful.

The effect of these Comanche raids was generally discouraging to would-be settlers of what was still Fannin County. One such aspirant, Edmiston Cox, had attempted to settle on the Blackland Prairie in early 1842 as a member of Peters Colony, leaving Arkansas with about 30 men. On their way to what eventually became Allen, Texas, Cox passed the cabin of Daniel Dugan. The Dugan's son and a friend had been killed and scalped by Indians that attacked their home on July 27, 1841. As they passed the Dugan place, they saw the severed head of an Indian that had been killed by young Catherine Dugan soon after her brother's murder. Catherine and her sister had been home alone when an Indian had appeared on their property. After fatally shooting the Indian, the girls dragged his body to a chopping block and cut off his head, putting it on a pole, thereby fulfilling Catherine's promise to her dead brother. From that point on, Edmiston Cox's party was in constant fear of Indian attack. After locating a settlement near Little Elm, Cox and two men blundered into the aftermath of the murder of Dr. Calder in the spring of 1843 while on the way to Fort Inglish for supplies. Allen's settlement was completely abandoned as they had all fled, leaving Dr. Calder's body. Cox found out later that he had ridden right by where the body lay. He went back to his settlement near Little Elm and found that everyone had forted up, "scared nearly out of their wits." Indians had surrounded their stockade but eventually left.

In August of 1843 Jeremiah Muncey, with his wife and four children, had moved out to Rowlett Creek with Muncey's friend McBain Jameson, one of the very first settlers of Collin County. In late 1843 or early 1844, Indians attacked a community about three miles east of McKinney killing two of the Alred boys. Not long after this attack, William Rice, a survivor of the attack on McGarrah's settlement, took his son Joe along on a hunting trip with Leonard Searcy and his son Gallatin. Reaching Rowlett Creek, one of the men went into Muncey's camp, where he found that everyone had been massacred. Jeremiah Muncey and McBain Jameson were found lying face down, shot to death. Muncey's three-year old child had been held by his feet and swung head-first into a wall; his wife had fought to the death with a Bowie knife, her body horribly mutilated. Three other children were missing; one had escaped, running for help to the Throckmorton settlement: the other two were later found to have been killed by the Indians as they headed westward. An entire family had been wiped out.[3]

Terrified, Searcy and Rice frantically searched for their sons, only to find Joe Rice's mutilated body. Returning home to Wilson's Creek some ten miles away, they found that Gallatin Searcy had escaped the Indians and beaten them home. Gallatin told the men that he and Joe had been surprised while riding horses on the prairie by a party of Indians who pretended to be friendly. Several Indians had laid their guns on the ground and motioned for the boys to come closer. Two Indians then seized the bridles of their horses and attempted to drag the boys down; only Gallatin escaped by spurring his horse. Joe had been shot and scalped, bringing the total to seven settlers killed that day in Collin County. Attempts to apprehend the killers were unsuccessful. Finally, on October 7, 1844, President Sam Houston got the Penateka Comanches to attend a council at the Kichai village, along with the Caddos, Delawares, and non-hostile members of the Wichita tribes. After two days of negotiations, a treaty was signed, which was ratified by the Texas Senate on January 24, 1845. Most of the Indians kept to the treaty and relative peace ensued for the next three years. During that time the Caddos helped enforce the peace, sometimes acting as intermediaries with the still-hostile Wacos.

During this period of tribulation, settlement of the Blackland Prairie accelerated because of the advent of Peters Colony, the brainchild of a group of rather ordinary men from London, England, and Louisville, Kentucky, whose reach would eventually exceed their grasp of what was needed to operate a colonization scheme. Only one of the 11 Englishmen involved in its origination was known to have ever visited Texas; virtually nothing is known of the nine American originators, one of whom was W. S. Peters. William Smalling Peters and his cohorts proposed to settle a large area of North Texas by

Plat map of the projected town of Buckner if it was voted as the Collin County Seat. Prepared by early land surveyor Henry O. Hedgcoxe.

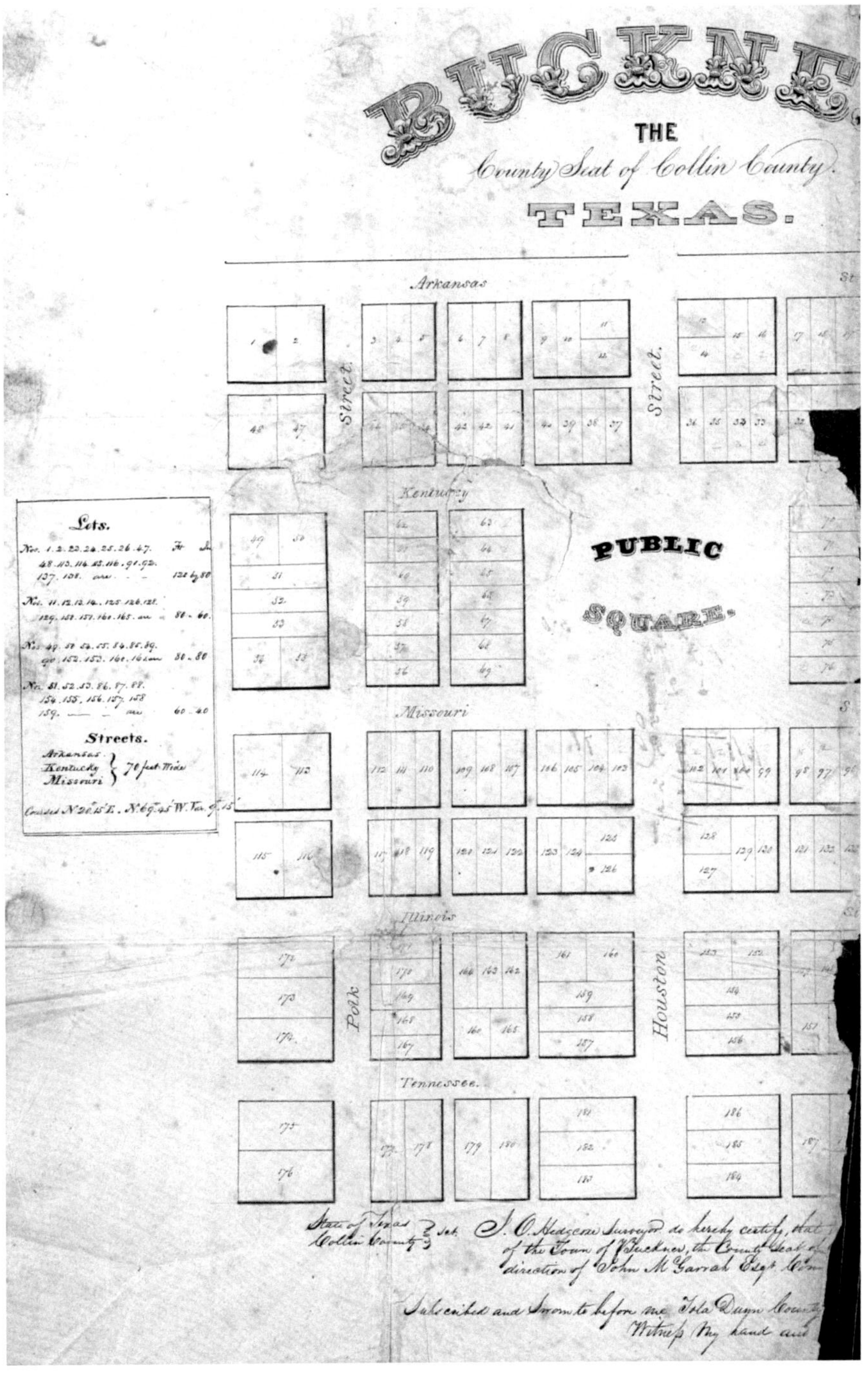

inducing immigration in a way similar to the Mexican empresario system—by offering free land to permanent settlers. Beset by Indian attacks and threats from its former owner, the Mexican government, the Republic of Texas was so fragile and vulnerable that it leapt at the chance for any influx of population that might strengthen its position. A law was passed on February 4, 1841, that allowed the Texan government to enter into an empresario contract. In doing so the Republic agreed to grant 640 acres of land to each family and half of that to each such single man over 17 years of age. After several false starts, what was to become the Texas Emigration and Land Company was formed and by January 1842 the first group of settlers left Louisville, Kentucky, for north Texas. By September 1842 there were 54 families in the colony; of these, 12 families abandoned the settlement and may have left to resettle in competing colonies elsewhere. In the aftermath of Dr. Calder's murder, by July of 1843 there seemed to be only 35 families left in the entire colony.

Above: Alfred Chandler, c. 1880.

Below: Collin McKinney, pioneer, minister and statesman.

The terms of the colony's contract required that 250 colonists be settled by July 1, 1844. With their dream in jeopardy, the colony's agent began to advertise in newspapers, and by July 1, 1844, they reported 381 colonists, the result of three years of work, during which virtually no improvement was made in the administration of the colony itself. To make matters worse, the Colony's settlers discovered that they were required to give one-half of their allotted land to W. S. Peters and Associates for expenses involved in securing the grant and for a cabin and supplies once they arrived in Texas. By 1844 the Republic of Texas was granting 640 acres of land to heads of families outside of the Colony, which further angered the members of Peters Colony, who complained to the State that the Texas Emigration and Land Company had not lived up to its promises. Texans gave up on the idea of being an independent Republic and joined the United States of America, becoming the twenty-eighth state on December 29, 1845. Attempts at introducing the grievances of the colonists to the state convention proved fruitless. In 1846 the Peters Colony area was organized by the State into four different counties, with Collin County officially coming into being on April 3. Peters Colony ceased to be a colony at that point and was forced into the role of land agent only. At the time of its creation in 1846, the entire population of Collin County was estimated at 150 people.

The McGarrah settlement where Dr. Calder had lost his life became known as Buckner and in 1846 it was one of two settlements in the entire county. On July 4, 1846, the county residents who could get to Buckner came to discuss the location of the new county's seat of government. John McGarrah's store was virtually the only place within 40 miles where any kind of merchandise could be purchased, so it was voted the county seat. On July 13th the following county officials were elected: Z. Roberts, chief justice; Moses G. Wilson, district clerk; T. Dunn, county clerk; King Custer, sheriff; John Fitzhugh, Godfrey Baccus, Peter Lucas, and John Wilson, county commissioners; William W. Butler and Jacob Baccus, justices of the peace, and William W. Butler, constable. The Baccus family had come to Collin County from Illinois at the inducement of Peters Colony in late September 1844 settling on Rowlett Creek near what is now Plano, joining the families of Hogan Witt and Samuel Young. They must have arrived sometime after the massacre of the Muncey family. The Baccus and Witt families are among the most colorful of the early Peters Colony settlers. Like most of the colonists, they were former residents of the Ohio River Valley, and like the Thomas Rattan family, they were slave owners who had left Greene County, Illinois to resettle in Texas, hoping to keep their slaves a little longer. Their family stories are emblematic of the changes that have swept the Blackland Prairie and its people.

By the end of 1846 the county seat of Buckner had a general store which also doubled as an inn, a blacksmith shop, a post office, and John L. Lovejoy's dry goods store—the first frame building. Collin County was still, as one settler put it, "a wild waste. Some feeble attempts had been made toward settlements, but they were scarcely more than widely separated dots on the boundless prairie."[4] When new settlers continued to arrive, they found, "clear streams with clear running water...wild flowers of every color and variety all around them, and wildlife in every direction...in the fall of the year, buffalo came to the watering places in great numbers and when given a scare, would stampede, making a noise like thunder." They found that the Blackland soil, composed of varieties of limestone-derived clay, was especially good for the growing of corn, wheat, sorghums, and hay—all forms of grass. It was not until later that cotton was grown in any quantity. Since the first killing frost does not occur in this land until November 11 and the last on March 28 on average, this leaves a growing season of 228 days—something unheard of in the Ohio River Valley. The land was excellent pasturage for grazing animals, and wild cattle roamed the prairie—the descendants of an early variety bred by Spanish settlers who would drive their herds into East Texas for grazing from their ranchos in Mexico. The great Texas cattleman Charles Goodnight said that these wild cattle looked like the little black bulls that fought in the bullrings of Mexico; the longhorn cattle commonly associated with Texas were brought later by the settlers from Kentucky. Most of the early settlers of Collin County were stock raisers first, and farmers second. Charles Goodnight's future partner in the cattle business, Oliver Loving, came to Collin County and settled in 1845.

As the Texas Emigration and Land Company was lax in its duty to secure land titles for Peters Colonists, ownership disputes were bound to occur. The first thing a new settler of the Blackland Prairie had to do was to provide shelter. If there was not an existing cabin in place, which was usually the case, they had to build one by cutting timber. There was plenty of timber to be had locally, but it was still considered a valuable asset. In 1847 Jacob Baccus, his sons Godfrey and Peter, Hogan Witt, Jonathan Brown, Samuel Brown, and Samuel Young were all sued in Collin County court by Alfred Slack of Missouri and ordered to appear in court at Buckner to answer for illegally cutting timber from Slack's property on Rowlett Creek. Apparently the disagreement was settled peacefully.

Another land dispute arose as to where the county seat should be located, as state law required it to be in or near the geographic center of the county. George White was appointed to survey the county in 1847 with November 1 set for site selection. White determined that geographic center was actually seven miles east of Buckner, so ultimately voters were given a choice between two potential new sites for the county seat: the William Davis homestead, which eventually became the town of McKinney, and another place called Sloanville, which has since disappeared. Only eleven people voted on November 1, and as the polls were set to close, ten votes had been counted for McKinney. Benjamin Baccus came in just before the polls closed and cast his vote for Sloanville, "just for devilment".

Counting Jacob Baccus' seven children, and the 1845 arrival of his brother Enoch and his sons, Thomas and Joseph Clark Baccus and his children, they were a force to be reckoned with. James M. McReynolds, who had settled in the county in 1843 and was appointed a county commissioner in 1848, appointed Peter Baccus as overseer of the road from McKinney to the seat of Denton County. Hogan Witt and Peter Baccus built a gristmill for people to grind their corn near the Allen and Lebanon road, and in 1850 the first Baptist church in the county was built near the mill on Rowlett Creek. On Christmas night, 1849, a ball was held to celebrate the opening of the courthouse built in the new county seat of McKinney; Jacob Baccus' daughter, Lucy, and Alfred Chandler led the grand march around the town square. The town had been named in honor of North Texas pioneer Collin McKinney, a drafter and signer of the *Texas Declaration of Independence* from Mexico.

Collin McKinney had been born in New Jersey in 1766 and was a participant of the general westward migration from the original thirteen colonies. By 1830 he and most of his relatives had relocated to Northeast Texas. After the Texas Revolution he was elected a delegate to the First, Second, and Fourth congresses of the Republic of Texas. Moving to the area of Fannin County that later became the Grayson-Collin County line, he and

The Wetzel brothers in Templar uniforms.

his son William organized a church on Hickman's Prairie in 1842. Soon after the creation of Collin County in 1846, he and Joseph Brice Wilmeth, who had arrived in the area with his family the previous year, founded the first church in Collin County. Later, the small congregation moved to a house one mile further south to an area that became known as Mantua. In 1848, J. B. Wilmeth organized a group at his home two miles north of McKinney, from which emerged the First Christian Church of McKinney. Beginning in 1848, J. B. Wilmeth and his children taught a free school, conducting classes in their home. It is a testament to the closeness of the Wilmeth and McKinney families that one of J. B. Wilmeth's thirteen children was named after Collin McKinney, considered by members of the Church of Christ a "Christian patriarch". Collin McKinney died on September 8, 1861, and was buried on land that would become the town of Van Alstyne in 1872, when the Houston & Texas Central Railroad bypassed Mantua.

George Washington Smith, pioneer veteran of the Texas War for Independence and the Mexican War.

The population of Collin County had reached 1,950 people in 1850, including 134 slaves. About half of the county was in Peters Colony, as well as roughly 66 percent of the population. The colonists had succeeded in getting the state government to pass a law on January 21, 1850, to remove the claims of W. S. Peters and Associates to the half-grants of land they intended to extract from the colonists. Further legislation in 1851 found that the Texas Emigration and Land Company had done everything in its power to comply with the terms of its contracts with the colonists. Henry O. Hedgcoxe, an Englishman, become the colony's agent and set up an office about four miles from McKinney in order to better explain the company's position to the colonists, who had grown tired of waiting for title to their lands. After much deliberation among the colonists, on July 16, 1852, a group of about forty men, "the best in the colony, men of age, influence and discretion" assembled in McKinney with the intent of raiding Hedgcoxe's office to confiscate his records.[5] The group was joined in McKinney by James M. McReynolds, chief justice of Collin County, and Sheriff James Read. Hedgcoxe was forced to leave the county and some of his records were confiscated and taken to Dallas, where they later burned in a courthouse fire. The rest of the records were sent to the land company's office in Louisville, Kentucky. Known as the Hedgoxe War, all the incident did was to slow the process of issuing land titles. Eventually the State of Texas intervened and gave the company 1,088,000 acres of land further west, and 640 acres to each head of a family that settled in the colony, with half that amount for single men.

With that nagging issue finally settled the residents of the county set about improving their living conditions. There was no industry at this point; the most mechanized operations being the gristmills used for grinding corn. Each settlement would typically build their own mill, which consisted of two wheel-shaped stones turned by oxen. It is believed that the first mill of this type was opened by John Wetzel in 1848; it was located at or near what is now 502 South Tennessee Street in McKinney. Each family was responsible for their own food which was easily

grown once the sod had been "busted" or broken. However, breaking the sod took time, for it was not the Johnson grass and ragweed that we have today—it was composed of native prairie grasses like sideoats grama, little bluestem and big bluestem that grew as high as a horse's belly. The turf it provided was a thick mat that was impenetrable; teams of oxen were needed for the initial breaking which could be undertaken once the area had been burned down to the roots. Even then it would be a year before the thick mat had rotted enough for the soil to be seeded. Once the sod was broken, it changed the ecosystem of the Blackland Prairie forever. Twenty-five to fifty acres of land was about the largest area that could be cleared and maintained by one farmer in the early days, which relegated them to subsistence farming. There were exceptions, however; William Forman II of Plano and his brother Joe jointly broke and fenced about 200 acres. Using slave labor, they were able to produce surplus corn which they distilled into whiskey. Opening a store and gristmill near Plano, they were able to sell whiskey and grind corn and wheat for the newer arrivals who had yet to make a crop.[6]

There were others who used slave labor to gain an early advantage over their neighbors, including the Brinlee family, early settlers of Red River County who had moved to Collin County in 1844. Settling at Stony Point near present-day Westminster and Blue Ridge, they were among the larger slave owners and became early cotton farmers during the 1850s. Hiram Carroll Brinlee would haul his cotton by wagon to New Orleans for shipment, making him perhaps the earliest commercial cotton producer in Collin County. His father Hiram opened a general store at Stony Point; his mother was Elizabeth Ann McKinney, a niece of Collin McKinney. The Brinlee family cemetery is five miles east of Melissa. It and the

Above: Until it was razed in 1941, the John Brice and Nancy Wilmeth homestead was located north of Highway 380 in McKinney on what is now Highway 5. In this October 1889 photograph both J. B. and his bride are seated in front of their house.

Left: Nancy Ferguson Wilmeth, January 1, 1807-January 14, 1892 and Joseph Bryson (Joe Brice) Wilmeth, September 11, 1807-January 15, 1892.

accompanying church are the only remnants of Stony Point, which remain near Brinlee Branch, a small creek between Altoga and Blue Ridge.

The relation of the Brinlee family to the McKinney family illustrates how tightly intertwined the pioneer families of the county were. The marriages of the children of Thomas Rattan, one of the few slave owners in the county before 1860 further illustrate how these marital relations would later complicate the legal and political situation. Harriet Rattan married Andrew Jackson Witt, Sarah Rattan married Carroll McKinney, Louisa Rattan married Hogan Witt, Mary Rattan married William Fitzhugh and Ann Rattan married James W. Throckmorton, who later became the most important political figure in Collin County. Through his marriage to Ann Rattan, J. W. Throckmorton was tied to the slave owing class represented by the Rattans, Brinlees, Witts, and their allies the Baccus and Forman families. This would later result in a moral crisis for Throckmorton that left his conscience torn and his loyalties divided.

Aside from the commercial farming operations of the Forman and Brinlee families, slaves were sometimes used in caring for the cattle that ran free on the open range, using specially trained dogs to round them up. Slaves were generally not trusted alone on horseback, as they could easily escape captivity, so they were kept on foot and were only chained when being transported for sale, or in captivity as the result of an escape attempt. The aftermath of one such attempt is recorded in the police court records of Collin County: James H. Lovejoy was paid a fee for "taking up a slave" and other fees for "keeping Negro from 25th March 1856 to the 4th of November 1856" and for "ironing Negro slave"—putting him in chains. In his duties as justice of the peace he had then run advertisements in the *State Gazette* and *Dallas Herald* giving notice of the runaway slave's capture, according to county records. Usually there was a reward offered by the owner for the return of the runaway slave. Slaves were also used in the breaking of wild horses to harness,

Illustration of "creasing" method of catching wild horses.

a dangerous activity. There were several herds of wild mustangs roaming the area known as Mustang Flats, the area around present-day Highway 380 and Preston Road, also known as "The Flats" of the Trinity Valley. It usually took several men to capture one wild horse, and they had to work in teams until the mustang finally tired enough to be roped—and then the fight began. Once the mustang was subdued enough to be brought back to the settlement, the slave was required to "break" the horse while penned in a corral.

By the mid-1850s there was a notable influx of slave-owning immigrants into Collin County, as noted by resident Elder Horn:

> Many immigrants are coming in from Missouri, Kansas, Iowa, etc. The fear that Kansas is to be a free state drives slavery-men to Texas. Missouri is alarmed at being surrounded by free states, and the slave owners are coming to Texas. The class of immigrants is much better than heretofore.

One of the immigrants just prior to the Civil War was South Carolinian John T. Coit. Among his papers are a document dated April 16, 1858, at Cheraw, South Carolina, the location of his family's plantation, which seems to be a checklist for "2nd Lieut. W. B. Smith" to prepare and send to "John T. Coit, Lieut. Col. 28th Regt." The list is a blank form for listing soldiers or muster roll, and an inventory of items that include copies of tactics and "Militia Law". It is unknown as to why Coit was being sent to Texas, but while on this trip, he received a letter dated May 13, 1858, asking him the favor of, "...bringing home with you two negroe [sic] men of mine now in Austin...." Working his way back north through the state, John Coit wrote his wife from Dallas on June 15, 1858 to inform her that he had "...just bought 320 acres of land in the Northern part of this county part lies in Collin County...on it is a beautiful mound from which you can see in one direction 40 miles—the county is thinly settled.... It is 2 or 3 miles E. of the S.E. corner of Denton County—and about 5 W. of the village of Plano." Before long Coit would permanently move his family from Cheraw, South Carolina, to Collin County. [7]

✧

Brothers Jim and Bob Carpenter of Plano pose with Armstead Hill and a horse-drawn plow in this studio photograph dated February 24, 1885.

At some point, John Coit made the following report on one of his early journeys through Texas, titled "Map of General Fertility":

> Although a reader of S. C. (South Carolina) while I have noticed communications from other portions of our state, I have seen none from the section known as Northern Texas—or the Wheat Region.... Nowhere throughout the wide extent of this beautiful and fertile belt—are there more advantages blended than in the region of which I propose to give in this paper an account.... This exceedingly rich soil through out the counties of Collin and Dallas, averages probably not less than three feet in depth.... Within this favored region the productions of different climes seem blended—the prairies of Illinois and Iowa not excelling it for small grain—and the richest uplands of Alabama or Mississippi in yeild [sic] of cotton—and the natural grasses of the prairies supporting horses sheep and cattle throughout the entire year....

It is not known for whom this undated report was intended, but a similar one written by J. W. Latimer for the 1859 Texas Almanac would be published on December 22, 1858, in the *Dallas Herald*:

LETTER FROM JOHN COIT TO HIS WIFE CATTIE, JUNE 18, 1858.

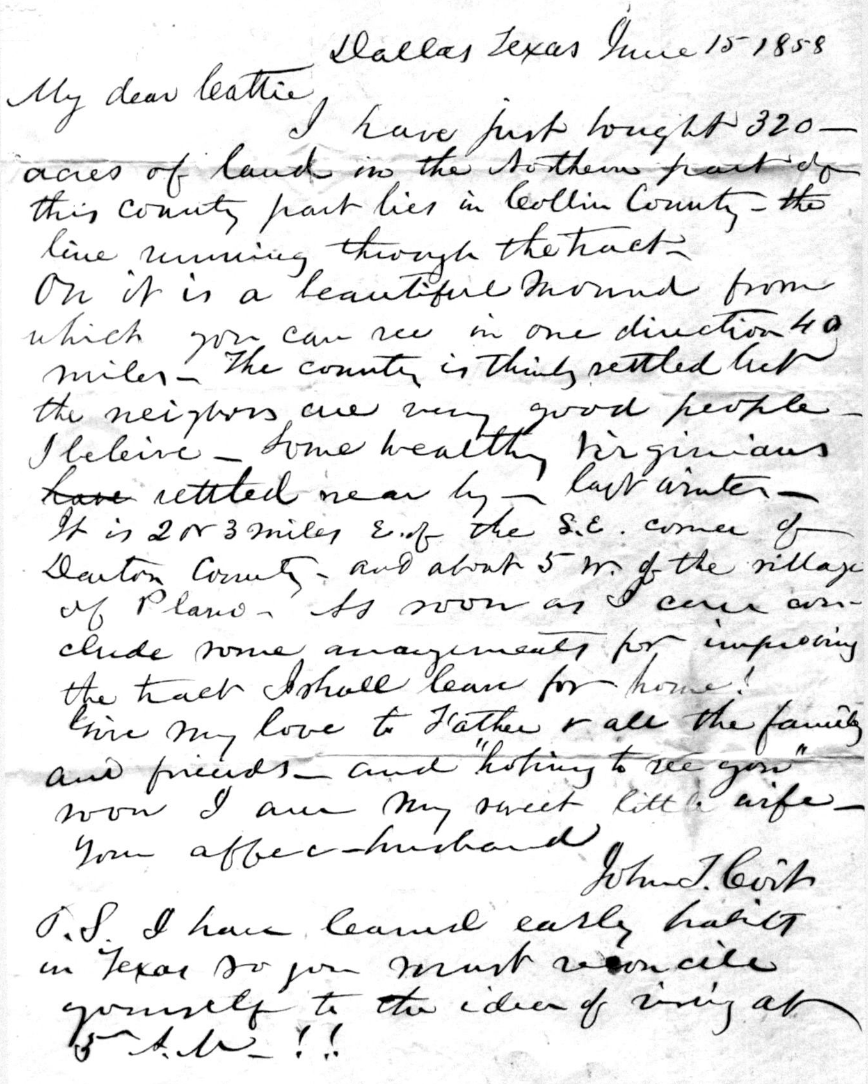

Dallas Texas June 18 1858
My dear Cattie,
I have just bought 320—
acres of land in the Northern part of
this county part lies in Collin County—the
line running through the tract—
On it is a beautiful mound from
which you can see in one direction 40
miles— The county is thinly settled but
the neighbors are very good people—
I believe— Some wealthy Virginians
~~have~~ settled near by— last winter—
It is 2 or 3 miles E. of the S.E. corner of
Denton County— and about 5 W. of the village
of Plano— As soon as I can con-
clude some arrangements for improving
the tract I shall leave for home!
Give my love to Father & all the family
and friends— and "hoping to see you"
soon I am my sweet little wife—
Your affec—husband
John T. Coit
P.S. I have learned early habits
in Texas so you must reconcile
yourself to the idea of rising at
5 A.M.—!!

Dallas, Texas, June 18, 1858

My dear Cattie,

I have just bought 320—acres of land in the Northern part of this county part lies in Collin county—the line running through the tract—on it is a beautiful mound from which you can see in one direction 40 miles—The country is thinly settled but the neighbors are very good people I believe. Some wealthy Virginians have settled near by—last winter. It is 2 or 3 miles E. of the S. E. corner of Denton County, and about 5 W. of the village of Plano. As soon as I can conclude some arrangements for improving the tract I shall leave for home! Give my love to Father & all the family and friends—and "hoping to see you" soon I am my sweet little wife—
Your affect—husband

John T. Coit

P. S. I have learned early habits in Texas so you must reconcile yourself to the idea of rising at 5 a.m.!!

✧

PHOTOGRAPH COURTESY OF THE DALLAS HISTORICAL SOCIETY.

THE WHEAT REGION AND WHEAT CULTURE IN TEXAS

Wheat, within a few years, has become one of the staple products of Texas, and its culture has grown in importance to the agricultural interests of the State little dreamed of ten years ago. To show the rapid increase in its production, it is only necessary to state that in 1850, according to the census of that year, only 41,725 bushels were grown in the State while it is safely estimated that in that portion of Northern Texas comprising the 16th Judicial District alone, namely, Collin, Grayson, Cook, Denton, Wise, Parker, Johnson, Ellis, Tarrant, and Dallas, there has been grown the past season more than 2,000,000 bushels, and that, too, with an almost minimum yield per acre. Ten years ago, wheat was cultivated in inconsiderable quantities, more as an experiment than otherwise, and at most, to furnish breadstuffs to those districts of the country inaccessible to market. It has thus been grown in quantities nearly sufficient for home consumption in some of the Red River counties for twenty years past. Indeed, its culture for this purpose was introduced into the prairies of Red River county by the first settlers, as early as 1833…

—J. W. Latimer

WHEN READY FOR MARKET

New flour may be manufactured ready for market from the 15th of May to 1st June—depending, in a measure, upon the season, which is six weeks in advance of Northern or Western flour, where the wheat does not ripen until July. This will give Texas a great advantage over all other wheat-growing regions. When facilities of transportation to market shall be afforded—when railroad connection to the Gulf is opened, wheat-growers in Northern Texas can have new, fresh flour in all the Southern markets if necessary, before the Northern wheat has ripened, and thus monopolize the trade several weeks, and command the highest prices. This will render wheat-growing in Texas a sure and remunerative business, so soon as our prairies are brought into communication with the Gulf....

Jefferson Davis, from his cabinet position as secretary of war (1853-1857) under President Franklin Pierce, would have had this information on the vital Texas wheat culture. An army traveled on its stomach, and wheat was not grown in any large quantity anywhere else in the South, so Texas would by necessity need to be in the Confederacy to insure a successful rebellion, whether the majority of the people wanted it, or not.

Collin County got its first newspaper, *The McKinney Messenger*, in February, 1859. *The Messenger* was soon to have local competition. John Henry Bingham came to Dallas in 1859 at the age of seventeen. He soon found work as a typesetter for the *Dallas Herald*, where his work was recognized. Soon, with the backing of Collin County residents Isaac Graves and Judge Muse, Bingham was able to purchase the *McKinney Enquirer*, whose operations were to be temporarily curtailed by the coming Civil War. On November 15, 1860, Abraham Lincoln was elected as President of the United States; by then many slave owners felt war was inevitable.

Above: John Henry Bingham, publisher of the McKinney Enquirer*.*

Below: Isaac Graves' home was once comparatively grand, but eventually fell into disrepair and was razed.

Since 1870 McKinney's African American community has had Ross Cemetery in which to bury its dead. Pecan Grove is located immediately to the north and contains the graves of many of Collin County's early families.

By August 31, 1860, James L. Read had been elected Collin County sheriff; the population of the county had grown to 9,246, of whom 1,047 were African-American slaves, which implies a significant influx of slave owners. The county records note the appointment of "Patter Rollers" for that session of court, whose job it was to patrol the county roads looking for runaway slaves. John Coit received the following letter from Eli Witt, dated January 9, 1861:

> Colonel Jno. T. Coit
> Sir
>
> The young ladies of McKinney are preparing a Secession Flag, to be raised prior to the day of Election, and are desirous that you should address them upon the subject of Secession. A dinner will be prepared by them, and they probably will present the Flag to a Union man with the request that he will hoist it....
>
> With the hopes that you will respond to the call, that you "will lead the blind by a way which they know not, and in paths with [sic] they have not known", and that you will acquit yourself of the duty assigned to you.
>
> We are, your humble servts
> G. G. Lyons
> Eli Witt

The "day of Election" was February 23, 1861, the day the citizens of Texas were to be allowed to vote on the Ordinance of Secession, which would take Texas out of the Union and into the Confederate States of America. Asking a Union man to raise a Secession flag was one way to put him on the spot—to make him publicly declare himself either for or against secession. The wrong answer, in front of witnesses, could be a fatal mistake. Many of the Unionists in North Texas were old settlers like James Read and James McReynolds, Peters Colonists and participants in the Hedgcoxe War. One settler described the loyal men in North Texas thusly:

> The most of them were oald settlers in this county, an had fought the Indians from there door steps. An tha did not want to be crouded backon the back seat by a fiew new comers that was trying to take the lead an run the country [sic]. [8]

James M. McReynold's widow later wrote a letter to military officials that Sheriff Read had been elected sheriff of Collin County by the Union men, had voted against the Ordinance of Secession, had hoisted a Union flag and had given a Christmas day dinner in 1860 in support of the Union. By the time of Eli Witt's letter to John Coit, Sheriff Read was firmly identified as a Union man in Collin County. This was to have tragic consequences for Collin County during the coming Civil War.

One of the first granaries that Charles B. Moore built in Collin County still exists today, minus its siding and a contemporary roof structure.

PHOTOGRAPH COURTESY OF BRYAN LEAN.

Chapter III

Civil War

One Collin County witness to the incidents leading up to the vote on Secession was Charles B. Moore. Born August 6, 1822, in Sumner County, Tennessee, Moore was a millwright and craftsman, skilled at designing and constructing gristmills and sawmills from the 1840s onward.

Moore left Tennessee for Texas in 1856. He was restless early in his life, and planned someday to buy land for farming and settle down. He and his brother Henry, found land near McKinney, Texas, and purchased it in 1857. They split their time between millwrighting and farming.

✧

A Civil War era cabinet card of Governor Sam Houston.

Outspoken on his disgust of slavery, Moore condemned it on moral grounds and criticized those who profited from it. When Texas voted to secede from the Union, Moore knew that his views would not allow him to declare his support for the Confederacy, and he left Texas for five years. He settled in Jerseyville, Illinois, near St. Louis. In December of 1866, Moore returned to his farm in McKinney, staying out of the way of Reconstruction Era politics.

Brother Henry Moore joined the Confederacy after hearing future governor James Throckmorton speak on the Square in McKinney. He fought in Arkansas with the cavalry.

Charles and Henry's younger brother, Josephus, still living at home in Tennessee, joined the Volunteers and fought in the war. Union forces captured him in the battle for Fort Donaldson. He contracted tuberculosis in a Union prison and died on June 30, 1865, in his home in Fosterville, Tennessee.

Charles Moore died on November 25, 1901, on his homestead near Chambersville, Collin County, Texas. He left behind comprehensive journals of his experiences, especially those capturing the feelings of Collin County residents voting on Secession.

Feb 1861 — Sat 23rd

To Paris in a buggy with Aleck Mehane to vote against Secession. Mutch excitement. The secession flag with 13 stars hoisted on a high pole. The Disunionists came into town with their flag at the head of the procession but the Union procession was 2 or 3 times as long & had two Union flags. Secession was voted down by 87 votes in town.... The secessionists admit the county has gone for Union.

Sun 24th

The probability now is that all North Texas has voted against Secession but I think Texas has most likely voted herself out of the Union.

March 1861 — Sat 2nd

This day the Texas Convention probably declares or pronounces us out of the Union but I feel like it is a farce. I think I'll live in the United States of America yet.

Only 18 counties out of 122 in the State of Texas had majority votes against Secession; one of those voting to stay in the Union was Collin County, by a vote of 948 to 405, largely due to the efforts of its' State Senator, James W. Throckmorton, son of the founder of Throckmorton's settlement. Like Governor Sam Houston, whom he loyally supported, Throckmorton had worked for two years against secession; yet, after Texas formally joined the Confederacy on March 5, 1861, Throckmorton was one of the first in Collin County to enlist in the Confederate forces. On September 18, 1861, county officials appropriated funds of $1,545 each for payment to the members of Captain Bowen's Mantua Company and Captain J. W. Throckmorton's Company of Volunteers, which had disbanded in August after securing forts in Indian Territory. These men were fighting for their families, neighbors and friends more than for the cause of slavery. Muster rolls of the Confederate forces show more than 1,500 names of Collin County men enlisted. Many of them joined the Sixth Texas Cavalry in Missouri as did Throckmorton.

CITIES IN COLLIN COUNTY

	Votes For Secession	Votes Against Secession
Baccus	5	25
Farmersville	62	106
Hamptons	1	74
Lebanon	14	71
McKinney	124	348
Mantua	15	80
Maxwell	57	4
Millwood	41	17
Plano	55	18
Smiths	0	41
Weston	31	164

James L. Read had married Sarah Jane Wilmeth, the oldest daughter of J. B. Wilmeth's brother, but he did not serve in the Confederate forces, staying home to act as County Sheriff instead. Records indicate that he no longer personally attended sessions of county court, but spent his time instead in the District Court. His rivals alleged that he acted as sheriff in order to avoid service in the Confederate forces. James W. Throckmorton was discharged from military service on September 12, 1863, because

✧

Civil War Reunion at Kirkpatrick house, c. 1908. Kirkpatrick held annual Confederate reunions from 1883 to 1941. The house exists to this day on Parker Street in McKinney. Elder R. C. Horn is in back center, in white suit with the book.

of recurring health problems and did not return to service until near the end of the war. He was somewhere in Texas when the only Civil War battle that occurred in Collin County took place in early 1864 between Quantrill's Missouri Partisan Rangers and a small group of Collin County residents.

William Clarke Quantrill claimed sanction under the Confederate Partisan Ranger Act, which authorized certain guerrilla activities, and apparently had received a regular Confederate commission as a captain. However, like almost all of the Missouri bushwhackers, he operated outside of the Confederate chain of command. Considered by even some Confederates a terrorist, he led a band of 400 mounted guerilla fighters.[1] Among his men in 1863 were Jesse and Frank James, Cole Younger, and future Collin County resident Francis Marion "Tuck" Hill. On August 21, 1863, Quantrill and his men attacked the town of Lawrence, Kansas, where they killed as many as 200 men and boys, many of whom were unarmed citizens who were executed in front of their mothers, sisters, daughters and wives.[2] The news of this massacre was carried in northern newspapers that sometimes found their way to Union sympathizers in Texas. Men in Collin County like James L. Read and other Unionists prayed for the end of the war; others had already gone into exile.

Many Collin County residents had hopes of being rescued by Union General James G. Blunt who had an inflated opinion of himself as he had recently defeated rebel troops in Missouri and in Indian Territory. Blunt was on his way to Texas when he ran into Quantrill's force and had his troops cut to pieces on October 6, 1863. Blunt barely escaped with his life and left his Regimental flag behind on the field of battle, where it was picked up by Quantrill's men and taken to Texas. On October 23, half of Quantrill's men made a triumphant entrance into Bonham, parading Blunt's flag around the town square. Quantrill seems to have stayed in Sherman, Texas, north of Collin County, but his men fanned out across North Texas, creating havoc as they went. On December 23, 1863, four Missouri men associated with Quantrill attacked a farmhouse near Millwood in Southeastern Collin County. The four men were brothers named Calhoun, and they tortured John Lackey, the elderly man whose home they had invaded, hoping to induce him to give them money. When the Calhoun brothers finally realized that Mr. Lackey had no money, they killed him in front of his wife.

James McReynolds, the old and trusted pioneer citizen of Collin County, was a neighbor of Lackey's and a cousin of County Sheriff James L. Read. He rode to McKinney and convinced his cousin that the Calhouns had committed the murder. Sheriff Read then learned that the Calhoun brothers would be at a dance in Collin County. Read was able to approach one of the Calhoun brothers at the dance, who was probably full of liquor as well as big talk; he bragged about killing an old man named Lackey. When asked who their next victim would be, Calhoun answered, "old man McReynolds." With this information Sheriff Read was able to gather a posse and set a trap for the four men, and they captured three of them between Millwood and Farmersville on December 29, 1863. Two of the Calhoun brothers were killed and the other escaped, heading straight for Quantrill's camp in Grayson County. Infuriated, Quantrill elected to wait for events to unfold. On February 8, 1864, James L. Read and three other men were arrested for murder. At his trial on February 16, evidence was presented that exonerated Sheriff Read, and he was found not guilty. Military records indicate that Quantrill had been

While in Farmersville, Cole Younger a notorious outlaw and member of Quantrill's Raiders posed with a group of Confederate Veterans in front of the Cole Younger Show around 1902.

✧

A 1983 view of Isaac Graves' home shows a maintained yard and home. Graves frequently hosted Jesse and Frank James, as well as Cole Younger.

ordered on February 15 to cross the Red River into Indian Territory, but did not comply. After the verdict Quantrill and sixty men came to McKinney looking for Sheriff Read.

Sometime around February 22 Quantrill's men took up quarters in the Tucker Hotel on the northwest side of the square; James Read and thirteen men stayed on the southwest corner. When he realized how outnumbered he was, Read withdrew his men and took refuge in Wetzel's gristmill on what is now South Tennessee Street. Quantrill's men began firing in midmorning with rifles and continued into the evening hours. Read and his men had shotguns that could not reach Quantrill's men. The fusillade killed all of Read's horses and wounded many of his men. Under cover of darkness, Read and his men escaped. When Quantrill realized this, he and his men went to Read's empty house, which they burned to the ground. Quantrill then went back to Sherman, where on February 24 he addressed a letter to Thomas C. Reynolds, the Confederate Governor of Missouri living in exile at Marshall, Texas. Quantrill received two more letters from Reynolds at Sherman on March 5 and March 10.[3]

Read's wife and children had sought refuge with McReynolds at Four Mile Prairie in Van Zandt County, a Norwegian settlement with Unionist sympathies. They all met at the home of Read's mother-in-law, Nancy Holcomb Wilson. They were safe for only a brief time, and were arrested by "Patter Rollers" at Four

Mile Prairie on May 15. Quantrill and his men had already left Texas, crossing the Red River into Indian Territory on April 6, according to military records posted from Bonham. A mob of Confederate sympathizers took Read, McReynolds, and a previously uninvolved relative named Joseph Holcomb to Tyler, Texas, where they were lynched on May 18 after a mock trial. A witness said that before he was hung, Read told the mob, "I have been hunted and persecuted for my sentiments ever since the state seceded. I never fought against the state. My house was burned over the heads of my family in the town where I live. I am an honest man and served the country. I had to fly by night, with my wife and seven children to Van Zandt, and they hounded me out of that." Then he was hung.

James McReynolds, described as being about six feet, two inches tall, weighing about 270 pounds, was hung next. His son Sam, a Confederate soldier stationed nearby at Camp Ford, heard about the mock trial and raced to save his father, only to find him hanging from a tree. Holcomb was hung last, and was visibly shaken, almost inconsolable with grief and fear, as he had not been involved in any shooting anywhere; he was a resident of Van Zandt County. In Collin County the local Confederate government and its sympathizers did their best to cover up the affair. The county records do not mention James L. Read's demise or that of James McReynolds, one of the men responsible for laying out the town site of McKinney, and a pioneer resident since 1843.

The site of the triple lynching is now known as Confederate Avenue, within the city limits of Tyler on what was once the Canton Road. After the end of the war, eighteen men were indicted for the lynching; during the trial it became apparent that one of the leaders of the lynch mob was Van Zandt County man Bol Hubbard. Although he was acquitted in the winter of 1866, Hubbard was later found tied to a tree and shot full of holes sometime in April 1869; the sons of Read and McReynolds were suspected of committing the crime. James McReynolds was buried in Kaufman County, where he had relocated shortly before his death. James L. Read was reburied for the third time in Pecan Grove Cemetery in McKinney after 1870. As of this writing there is not a single plaque or memorial in Collin County to James L. Read or James M. McReynolds, two real pioneers of Collin County.

This 1934 triptych by Frank Klepper shows a company preparing to march off to the Confederate Army as the women present them with a flag. The body of General Ben McCulloch lies in the casket. McCulloch had been killed at the Battle of Pea Ridge and was being taken to Austin for burial.

CHAPTER IV

THE CATTLEMEN

✧

Longhorn immortalized in bronze can be found in Dallas, Frisco, and other locales, reminding North Texans of the famed animals' place in history.

PHOTOGRAPH COURTESY OF TXDOT.

The Blackland Prairie was the birthplace of the great cattle industry of America, which was dominated by the State of Texas during the industry's glory years from 1866-1892. This rich soil region is bounded by the Red River on the north, Hopkins County to the east; Collin County to the west, and then tapers southwestward to San Antonio. Settlement concentrated in the wooded eastern portion of the state, and the Blackland Prairie to the west was open range grazing land. Under laws of the Republic, any unclaimed land was public land and could be used by anyone that occupied it. It was a matter of driving one's cattle to a range before anyone else. Occasionally fights would occur over the use of waterholes for livestock; the first murder in Hopkins County was said to be the result of such a dispute.

Collin County was an early center of the Texas cattle industry because for a time most of the livestock in the state were driven to market via the Sedalia Trail. Also known as the Shawnee Trail, it followed an Indian route that had been adapted by early settlers who called it the Texas Road. It led from the rangelands in southern and southwestern Texas past Austin, Waco, and Dallas. From Dallas it entered the southwestern portion of Collin County along what is now Preston Road and passed by the town of Lebanon, where cattle pens were maintained. Passing two miles west of Rhea's Mills the road led north to the town of Preston in Grayson County on the Red River.[1] It was near Preston that the cattle would ford the river on their way to their ultimate destinations at Sedalia, Missouri, and points as far north as Chicago, Illinois. This trail had been in limited use in the 1840s by settlers like Henry Cook, who drove 100 cattle northeast on it in 1846, but it began to attract greater attention in 1850 as more and larger herds were driven along this route. By 1854 the Shawnee Trail was recognized as an important commercial byway; in June of that year Captain Randolph Marcy, an explorer and surveyor, estimated 10,000 Longhorn cattle were driven to Missouri and Illinois via the trail through Collin County[2].

Cattle from Texas made it as far east as New York, by way of Chicago, in 1853. However, in the 1850s Kansas cattlemen became hostile to the Texas cattle drives, as the Longhorns carried ticks that spread what became known as *Texas Fever*. The Texas Longhorn was immune to the fever, but not so the Kansas livestock, which died in large numbers. Soon demand in the eastern markets and the lure of sizable profits overcame any fears the Texas cattlemen had of the Kansas settlers. In 1857 former Collin County resident Oliver Loving drove a herd from Palo Pinto County through Collin County to the market in Missouri, earning a profit of $36 per head. Encouraged by his success, the following year he sent another herd northward along the trail. Cattle drives north began to slow in 1860 due to the anticipation of Civil War, but it was only the legitimate business that was affected.

✧

PHOTOGRAPH COURTESY OF THE FRISCO HERITAGE MUSEUM.

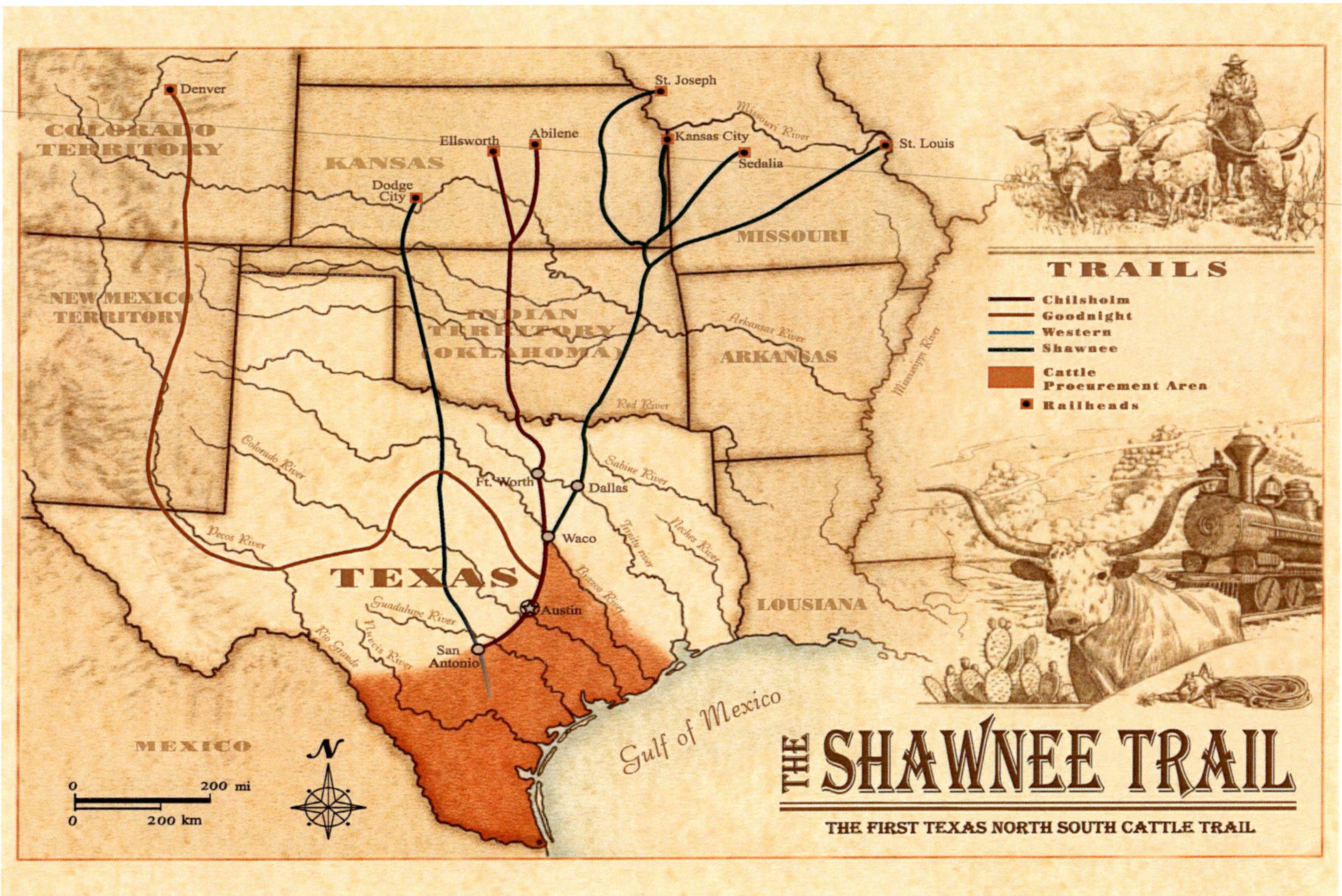

Stealing cattle was rampant, as the most punishment a thief would get was a $20 fine. Usually the thief was allowed enough time to steal more cattle to pay his fine. Stealing was easy because of the open range method of cattle raising, in which the owner branded a yearling calf and released it upon the unfenced range to feed itself, hoping he would see his property in the next year's roundup. A thief profited from this system in two ways: he could find a branded animal and change the brand by altering it with a hot iron, thereby claiming it for himself, or the thief simply put his brand on an unbranded yearling before the real owner even knew the calf had been born. As enforcement of the weak law was virtually non-existent, it became commonplace to settle these ownership disputes out of court by the knife, pistol, shotgun, or rifle. Towns like Lebanon became wild places that timid people avoided. For others in the cattle business, or for merchants and saloonkeepers that catered to the cattlemen, it was a magnet. One of the ancestors of United States President Lyndon Baines Johnson moved to Lebanon in 1851 to become a cattle raiser.

An unknown cowboy in well-worn chaps demonstrates the fashions of the day.

During the Civil War there was a substantial illegal trade in cattle. Collin County was in the center of the breadbasket of the Confederacy and astride the trail that carried beef to its soldiers. Once Missouri fell to Union forces, New Orleans became the alternate shipping point for Texas cattle until it too was taken in May 1862. It was then that cattle smuggling from North Texas into Union territory began in earnest. With most of the able-bodied men away at war, cattle stealing became even easier, with the added incentive of Yankee gold or silver in place of worthless Confederate paper. Stealing was not always necessary; counterfeit Confederate money was sometimes used to acquire Texas cattle that were then sold in occupied New Orleans as late as April 1863. The police court records of Collin County make reference to counterfeit Confederate money being passed in the area.

Indians across the Red River became willing intermediaries in the illegal trade with the Union. On August 6, 1864, the Kansas-based *Emporia News* reported that 12,000 cattle had been stolen from Texas that year and sold to Union troops in Kansas, Missouri, and Arkansas. By 1864 an elite unit of Confederate troops known as the Graham Rangers had been formed to police northeast Texas for illegal activity, led by Captain Courtes B. Sutton of Red River County. Sutton wrote the Adjutant General's office on June 15, 1864, that large droves of cattle were passing through Collin, Hunt, and Hopkins counties and that cattle were being carried into enemy lines. "I conclude", wrote Sutton, "that there has been smuggling going on by a set of men who have an allegiance to the South." Although Sutton noted that there were large numbers of deserters in Collin County, he absolved them of the illegal cattle speculation. One of the men with allegiance to the South who was also responsible for arresting the illegal trade was General James W. Throckmorton of McKinney, who was commanding the First Frontier Regiment. In a December 9, 1864 letter to Texas Governor Pendleton Murrah, Throckmorton wrote, "…Texas renegades & Jayhawkers & Indians are stealing cattle from our border & supplying the federal forces in Ark. & Kansas." The trade was never broken, and by the end of the Civil War there emerged a small group of Texas cattlemen who had done quite well for themselves, due in part to a law passed in 1862 that exempted cattlemen from military service. Most of the former Confederate soldiers returned from distant battlefields to find their farms and ranches stripped of everything, including livestock. Families like the Slaughter and Waggoner found themselves "short of good money, but long on cattle."[3] Eventually men from both of those families would become the wealthiest citizens in Texas.

By early 1866 C. C. Slaughter had driven a herd of cattle from Palo Pinto eastward to Jefferson, Texas, a riverboat town on the Louisiana border. Fortunately for the Confederate veterans, the free-range cattle that had not been captured or sold had bred like rabbits and were running wild on the prairie, waiting for the longest rope and fastest branding iron to claim them. The legitimate trade on the Sedalia Trail resumed after the war. On July 24, 1867, Elder Robert Cannon Horn, W. M. Collins, Joel Collins, and Collin McKinney Wilmeth drove fifty horses from Collin County to Colbert's Ferry on the Red River, where they crossed into Indian Territory on their way to Sedalia. Horn made a profit of $100 on his share and used the money to continue his education in Kentucky before returning home to preach the gospel in McKinney. William and Joel Collins, Dallas County men, later became members of the Sam Bass gang of outlaws. In an extraordinary series of letters, Mrs. Henrietta Knight wrote her husband John from their home in "Plano Collin Co Texas 4 miles South of Lebanon" while he was trailing cattle to Missouri and Chicago, from 1868 until December 1870. From her letters, one gets a sense of the loneliness and fear she had for her spouse on his dangerous journeys. Her letter of October 8, 1868 to him spoke of "…dread lest you will be like other trading men get so you will not care for your home and family I want to die before that time comes if it ever should…."[4] John A. Knight wrote his last letter from the trail at Baxter Springs, Kansas on December 18, 1870, that "I have recived 2 leters from you one of them trubled me a great deal Retta if my absence causes you so much trouble or to inger your helyth I shall never leave you again [sic]." He had delivered 200 cattle for shipment by rail that day to Kansas City.

Mrs. Knight's concerns were understandable; the Kansas cattle towns were wild and predisposed to separate a Texas cattleman from his money in any way possible. Gambling, prostitution and alcohol were the attractive nuisances, some of which are alluded to in a letter sent from Collin County by H. M. Parvin to his friend George M. Slaughter in Alabama in 1869:

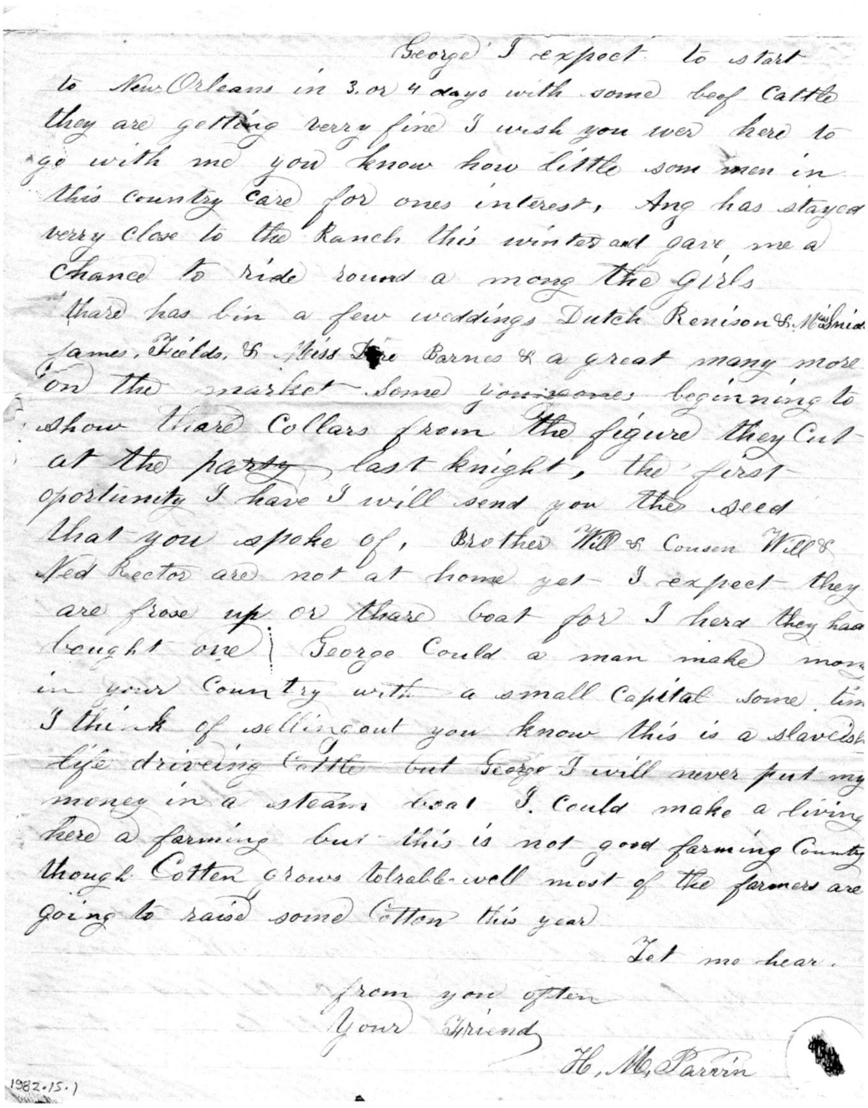
George I expect to start
to New Orleans in 3 or 4 days with some beef Cattle
they are getting verry fine I wish you wer here to
go with me you know how little som men in
this country care for ones interest, Ang has stayed
verry Close to the Ranch this winter and gave me a
Chance to ride round a mong the girls
thare has bin a few weddings Dutch Renison & [illegible]
James Fields & Miss [illegible] Barnes & a great many more
on the market Some youngones beginning to
show thare Collars from the figure they Cut
at the party last knight, the first
oportunity I have I will send you the seed
that you spoke of, Brother Will & Cousin Will &
Ned Rector are not at home yet I expect they
are frose up or thare boat for I herd they had
bought one | George Could a man make mon[ey]
in your Country with a small Capital some tim[e]
I think of sellingout you know this is a slavesh
lyfe driveing Cattle but George I will never put my
money in a steam boat I Could make a living
here a farming but this is not good farming County
though Cotten Grows tolrabl-well most of the farmers are
going to raise some Cotton this year
Let me hear
from you often
Your Friend
H. M. Parvin

1982.15.1

✧

A portion of one of Parvin's letters to Slaughter. The beautiful handwriting is typical of the day and shows a certain level of education.

✧

Left: This rocky outcrop was supposedly a hangout for Bass's gang while in nearby Denton County.

Right: This photograph of Sam Bass and his gang was taken in the summer of 1876 in Dallas, Texas. From left to right, back to front: Sam Bass, John E. Gardner, Joe and Joel Collins.

I saw a man from Cansas City day before yesterday that I was acquainted with. He wants to go in with us & furnish beef to supply the towns of Cansas City which will be 12 or 15 head per day. I expect to drive to Cansas next spring if I don't I will sell at home. I think the demand for cattle will be better than last spring. Stock is doing well as I ever saw them at this time of the year. The most trad we have had in the country now is the mule trade bying for the cotton industry.

George have you picked me out that sweet heart yet that you promised to. I have saw yours often that Nat Rector gave to you. She is ready when ever you call for her so far as I know.... George have you heard from your little Cansas gal yet. I have never wrote to them. I did not think I was the proper wone to write to them for they did not take on over me like they did you. No go with me to the watermelon patch...[5]

By 1870 changes were coming to Collin county; the *Weekly State Journal* reported in December 1, 1870, that "...a continuous stream of immigrant trains well provided with handsome outfits, fine horses and mules, and painted wagons" was seen heading into the northern Blackland Prairie. The article further describes "...a total of nearly one thousand wagons, for the most part freighted with families of sturdy children, and intent upon settling on the cheap and fertile wheat lands of Texas."[6] Many, it said, "...had located in Collin County." Davis Hester was one such immigrant from North Carolina who wrote a letter on May 4, 1870, from Collin County to his brother and sister, describing "...the richest landed & most beautiful country I have ever seen." He did complain that land and food prices were high in the heavily settled areas, "...owing to the great emigrations to this country last fall & winter." He noted, "There are immense herds of cattle horses & mules on the prairies & in some places large flocks of sheep.... They failed one or two years here in the wheat crop since but few sow it but chose to raise cotton buy flour & haul it. What wheat there is is looking very well & will soon be to harvest."[7] Cotton would eventually replace wheat as the major cash crop in Collin County, but the tax assessment published by the *McKinney Messenger* on June 18, 1870, shows 12,930 horses and mules, 22,799 cattle, and 5,535 sheep.

The influx of so many settlers starting farms began the decline of open range cattle grazing, but it was not the end of the cattle business. Rollie C. Burns, who had lived in Collin County from 1860 to 1867, came back to Weston in August 1873 to find work as a cowboy. Here he met J. W. Wilson, who had acquired a small herd with the ambition of building a ranch on the open range along the Red River. During the one year Burns worked for Wilson, he reported that Wilson and his men stole nearly 1,000 cattle. Shortly after Burns quit in August 1874, Wilson killed his first man; "It was only a starter for him though, as I understood he marked up several notches on his gun after that."[8] Criminal records across the State of Texas confirm this was so: J. W. "Bud" Wilson was indicted in Clay County in 1875 with "William Smith" for murder, and a reward was offered for their capture. Soon the press referred to him as "Wild Bill" Wilson and noted his uncanny ability to escape from any handcuffs or chains. The cattle inspection records in Montague County, the point at which herds were inspected on the Chisholm Trail before they crossed the Red River show numerous herds owned by Wilson. The cattle business had become a race to the top, with the winners becoming wealthy enough to buy their way out of prison. John William Wilson became a wealthy and powerful cattle baron, never serving prison time for the murders attributed to him.

The Sedalia Trail closed in 1874 with the advent of the opening of the Chisholm Trail further west, away from the settled areas. In 1872 the Houston and Texas Central Railroad came through Collin County, inaugurating another wave of immigration. Twenty-one year old James A. Brooks arrived in McKinney by train from Kentucky on January 1, 1877, to see his cousin Joe Darnell, who had established the Cottage Hill community. "I was again ushered into a hunter's paradise" wrote Brooks, "The bobwhite and the prairie chicken were in abundance."[9] In the spring he ventured into the open range, which now began in far western Collin County, meeting and making friends with Bob and Frank Hickman, who "...ran a successful cowboying company in Collin

Isaac Crouch's Furniture Store on Louisiana Street in McKinney, between 1877 and 1879. In front of the store, from left to right are: Jesse James, Isaac Graves, Isaac Crouch, unknown (possibly a Younger family member), Frank James, Tuck Hill, unknown, and Allen Parmer.

Left: William Alexander Rhea, founder of Rhea Mill community and mill and an early cattleman.

Right: Edward Rollin Stiff married Mary Margaret McGarrah of Buckner.

County not far from Pilot Point, especially famous for busting bronchos and organizing cattle drives up to Kansas." It was on Hickman's Prairie at a horse race that Brooks met Sam Bass, who had the fastest horse—a good thing for him, as he was already a noted cattle thief. Later Bass became a noted train robber, holding up the train at Allen, Texas, on February 22, 1878, committing the first such crime in the state. Bass was killed by Texas Rangers at Round Rock in Williamson County on July 21, 1878. In the spring of 1878, James Brooks bought a 116 acre tract on Wilson Creek, becoming neighbors of the Hickman family until the cattle trade beckoned him further west. Brooks later became a Texas Ranger Captain.

The *McKinney Weekly Enquirer* trumpeted in its February 2, 1878, issue that "Collin is destined to be the banner county in the state for fine stock, as she is in many other respects. Very nearly all our farmers are dispensing with their scrub stock and procuring that of a better class." The county seems to have led the way in the breeding of short horned stock, an improvement over the native Texas Longhorn. The *Victoria Advocate* had noted in April 14, 1877, that "...such animals are marketable one year before our native stock attain their full growth, and will be found less wild and troublesome to manage." This breed was more adaptable to the fenced-in pastures that spelled the end of the open range.

C. C. Slaughter was also an early advocate of short horned cattle and, in 1877, he and James Carroll Loving, the son of Oliver Loving, formed the Northwest Texas Cattle Raiser's Association to function as a cartel to protect the interests of big cattlemen. They began offering cash rewards for the capture and conviction of horse and cattle thieves that victimized Association members. This attracted prospective members, whose applications were voted on by the membership before they were allowed to join the Association. The Association's minutes show that William Smith and John Bland were awarded $400 for the capture of two horse thieves in 1881. Eli Calvin "Cal" Sugg became a member that year: he and his brother J. D. or "Ikard" Sugg were known to have killed seven men between them. The following year, William Smith's old employer

J. W. Wilson was allowed to join the Association, as was William E. "Billy" Washington, who had several indictments for cattle theft in Cooke County. In 1883, Allen Parmer was voted in for membership, as was C. C. Cannon, a former resident of Rockwall County with several indictments for cattle theft in Denton County. Cannon was connected to Sam Bass and his gang, and was killed by another cattleman later that year in Baylor County.

In 1883 Slaughter was put in charge of the development of a "protective force" of "detectives and inspectors" employed solely to protect the interests of Association members; their identities were never disclosed. These gunmen served at the direction of the Executive Committee. In 1884 a contingent of Collin County cattlemen was voted into Association membership: E. R. Stiff, F. M. Hill and J. C. Cameron. They joined the membership that included Fred Waite, a Chickasaw Indian rancher and former member of Billy the Kid's gang. New Association member Francis Marion "Tuck" Hill and his brother James "Woot" Hill were both veterans of Confederate William Quantrill's Missouri Partisan Rangers, and were cousins of Jesse and Frank James, whose sister Allen Parmer had married. The Hill brothers had settled in McKinney shortly after the Civil War without any repercussions from whatever role they may have played in the deaths of Sheriff Read and James McReynolds. Tuck and Woot married daughters of Albert G. Graves and were driving cattle for trade as early as 1871. John C. Cameron was also related to the Graves family by marriage. William A. Rhea of Rhea's Mills joined the Association in 1885, his acceptance signaling that he had attained a position of power and influence not only in his home in Collin County but in the rest of the state as well.

Allen Parmer was known to be an enforcer for cattlemen in Clay and Archer counties, where he was responsible for chasing "sod busters" off their land claims in order to keep the last remnants of the open range "free". Exactly what roles Tuck Hill and Fred Waite played in the Association are not known, for they were not Executive Committee members. Some of the Cattle Kings were also philanthropists, perhaps to sooth their consciences, and gave to a variety of causes. In 1870 Isaac Graves, E. R. Stiff, and three other men started the Pecan Grove Cemetery in McKinney. It is the final resting place of Governor James W. Throckmorton, Elder R. C. Horn and other early residents. E. R. Stiff also contributed by raising $1,000 for the construction of a new Male and Female School at McKinney in 1871. Countless other charitable and civic endeavors were initiated by the Cattle Kings during and after their golden age ended with the crash in cattle prices in 1892.

Former Quantrill's Raider James "Woot" Hill and a lady companion in Collin County.

Houston & Texas Central railroad bridge over East Fork of Trinity River, just north of McKinney, Autumn 1905.

CHAPTER V

RAILROADS AND RECONSTRUCTION

In 1870 Davis Hester had sent a letter from Collin County to his sister in North Carolina stating, "I would not be surprised if I can't find places in Texas that would suit me better than this." Although he was impressed with the land and its fertility, he complained of the scarcity of goods that had to be hauled by wagon from places as far away as Jefferson, a riverboat town more than 140 miles away: "The distance to market is an objection that I have in this part of the state. But I learn that we will soon have R. Roads here [sic].[1] Indeed, the arrival of the railroad was eagerly anticipated by all those who craved progress. In the dark years immediately following the end of the Civil War, especially from 1865-1869 when the Lee-Peacock Feud raged through Collin and three nearby counties in Texas, eastern capitalists were hesitant to finance railroads in Texas. In what became known as "The Second Civil War" Collin County's own Dow Witt, a member of Bob Lee's band of terrorists, was killed north of McKinney by the Collin County Sheriff George Wilson and a thirty-man posse on March 28, 1869; Bob Lee met a similar fate on May 24, 1869. With the leaders of the anti-government rebellion now dead or on the run, surplus Yankee capital came to Collin County in the form of the county's first bank, initially known as F. Emerson and Company. In 1873 the bank withstood a national financial market crash and was renamed the First National Bank of McKinney.[2]

After stopping due to the Civil War, construction resumed on the Houston and Texas Central Railroad, steadily expanding northward from Houston beginning in 1867. On July 16, 1872, the line reached Dallas, which up to that time was a tiny village. Towns everywhere in the state wanted the railroad to bring economic prosperity to their citizens, and vied for the chance. McKinney paid the railroad a bonus of $20,000, a substantial sum in those days, while its northern rival Sherman paid $50,000. On October 2, 1872, the train came to Collin County, ushering in a fifty year period of economic growth and expansion. Now that the ports of Houston and Galveston were connected by rail to Collin County, agricultural production boomed. In 1869, some 84,485 bales of cotton had been shipped from Galveston to markets around the world; by 1873 this number increased to 333,502 bales. Collin County itself produced 4,371 bales of cotton in 1870, a single standard bale weighing 400 pounds. In 1877 some 5,200 bales were received in McKinney, and that did not count those taken to Plano and Allen, the other railroad stops in the county. Plano reported 3,700 bales shipped the previous year.[3]

Along with the increase in agricultural production, the railroad brought more settlers, both average and infamous; the total number of county residents subject to poll tax rose from 3,521 in 1876 to 4,125 the following year. Others found the railroad convenient; outlaws like Frank and Jesse James and Cole Younger, famous train-robbers in their own right, made frequent visits to McKinney. John Henry "Doc" Holliday, a gambler and gunman later made famous for his connection with Wyatt Earp, often rode the Houston and Texas Central railroad from Denison through Collin County to the gambling dens in Dallas.

Telegraph service along the railroad also established more rapid communication with the rest of the state. By 1880 the county's population had grown to 25,983.[4] With the county's reputation as a farming and ranching center firmly established, more railroads built lines to

Horse drawn wagons loaded with cotton bales line up on Virginia Street in McKinney, c. 1885, heading east toward the railroad freight depot. Note the dirt street, the Houston & Texas Central railroad steam engine, and hundreds of 480-pound bales lined up on the freight loading dock. Once the farmer has unloaded his wagon, the team is parked behind the fence on one of the market lots and the driver goes off to the bank or stores to spend his earnings or pay his bills.

points in Collin County; The Missouri, Kansas and Texas in 1876, the Gulf, Colorado, and Santa Fe—known as "the cattleman's railway"—in 1886, the St. Louis Southeastern in 1887, and the St. Louis, San Francisco, and Texas in 1902.[5]

This last railway prompted the establishment in 1902 of the town of Frisco, Texas, which sprung from the farm of Francis Emerson, the McKinney banker. Electricity came to Frisco in 1913 and by 1914 its population was estimated at 1,000. Originally a shipping point for farmers, Frisco became a suburb of Dallas and grew to 33,714 by 2000. As of this writing the population is estimated at more than 102,000, making Frisco one of the fastest growing cities in the United States this decade—and it all started when the railroad came in 1902.

With the steam engine driving railroad traffic in Collin County to points across the state and beyond, in 1901 the first electric railway or "trolley" providing local transit in Texas began running between Denison and Sherman, a 10.5 mile trip taking thirty minutes. By 1909 the Interurban, as it was known, stretched from its original point in Grayson County through Collin County to Dallas. Its coaches were powered by electric motors from overhead cables

carrying 600 volts generated by substations along the line. By 1920 the Interurban carried nearly 4,000,000 passengers. By 1931 the interconnected systems of electric railways covered 518 miles in Texas, the longest stretch of which was the 226-mile-long Texas Electric Railway that served Collin County. With the end of World War II and America's growing love of the automobile, along with taxpayer funded highways, the Texas Electric Railway closed forever on December 31, 1948.[6] However the demise of the Interurban did not mark the end of mass transit by rail in Collin County.

On August 13, 1983, the Dallas Area Rapid Transit (DART) system was created when fifty-eight percent of the voters in fourteen cities and Dallas County voted in its favor. By September 1984 DART was running non-stop bus lines to Plano while it negotiated to purchase some of the old Houston and Texas Central Railroad

✧

Opposite, top: Motorman J. L. Bright stands in the doorway of McKinney Streetcar No. 151, c. 1913. There were four miles of streetcar track in McKinney on two routes, both of them heading west on Virginia Street with one turning north on College Street and the other north on Morris Street. They connected with the Interurban track on Kentucky Street. Streetcar service began December 1910 and ended November 1, 1926.

Opposite, bottom: Ollie Weaver Taylor is on duty at the Interurban Station, McKinney. The poster on the front of the counter advertises A Trip to Hitland, *a 1920 musical.*

Above: A Texas Traction Company postcard of the Sherman-Dallas Interurban at Van Alstyne Station.

Left: A Texas Traction Company postcard of the Sherman-Dallas Interurban bridge at Rowlette Creek.

✧

Above: The Interurban crossing the Missouri Kansas Texas Railroad on the Sherman-Dallas line.

Below: This "Frisco Viaduct" postcard shows both the Interurban and a steam engine.

Opposite, top: Interurban car No. 1 of the Texas Traction Company, inaugurates service on July 1, 1908. It is heading southbound (Dallas) on Kentucky Street in McKinney with the Collin County courthouse visible to the right of the car. Later, in 1908, the dirt streets within a block of the square were paved with brick. Interurban service extended from Denison through Dallas to Waco.

Opposite, bottom: Here two roads cross, one for cars and trucks, the other for trains. A sign for Dyers Drugs hangs on the bridge that frames a collection of houses in the background.

PHOTOGRAPH COURTESY OF TXDOT.

right-of-way prior to construction of the rail line. Impatient with perceived lack of progress, some area towns voted to pull out of the DART system, but in August 1989 voters in Plano opted to stay and wait for light rail service. It was not until June 14, 1996, that the first 11.2 miles of the DART light rail system went into operation in Dallas County; on August 10, 1996, voters in Plano again opted to stay within the DART system. The Center for Economic Development and Research at the University of North Texas in Denton estimated by February of 1999 that DART provided an economic boost to the Blackland Prairie of $3.7 billion and 32,000 jobs. Although the rails had not reached Collin County by late 1997, DART reported serving nearly 70 million passengers that year. On December 9, 1997, the DART Board voted to accelerate construction to Plano and to double track the rail line to handle more traffic. DART rail service reached Richardson and Plano six months ahead of schedule on December 9,

2002, completing stations at Downtown Plano and Parker Road. When oil prices spiked upward in 2008, DART reported its busiest month ever in May, with 10.3 million trips. Perhaps the greatest vindication of the dream of the Interurban came in March 2009, when DART was voted "Best Metro Americas" at the MetroRail Conference in London, England. The runners-up were the Metropolitan rail systems of New York, Washington, and Chicago.[7]

✧

Right: It is still possible to see a Texas electric railways interurban car at the Interurban Museum in Plano, Texas. Car 360, a railway post office and passenger car, is parked on what would have been the track. The original station and electrical substation make up the museum buildings.

PHOTOGRAPH COURTESY OF BRYAN LEAN.

Below: Utilizing parts of the right-of-ways of the Houston & Texas Central Railroad and Texas Electrical Railway, DART's Red Line Light Rail—the twenty-first century interurban—brings Collin County commuters home after a day in their Dallas offices. This is the George Bush Turnpike station, an example of an intermodal transportation facility, which includes an area for bus lines from Richardson, Plano, a university, and corporate campus and connections with a major toll road and expressway. Plano and DART have utilized the area under the toll road as parking for the station.

PHOTOGRAPH COURTESY OF BRYAN LEAN.

Chapter VI

Roads

Collin County grew to prominence due in part to having one of the earliest roads in the state and one of the earliest railroads. The Central National Road of the Republic of Texas had been cut from the Blackland Prairie in 1844 to connect with the National Road, an older road opened in 1840. Once the Central National and the National Road were linked, it created what was essentially an international highway between San Antonio and St. Louis that included Collin County.

McKinney's State Senator, James W. Throckmorton, a proponent of railroad expansion, successfully lobbied for the extension of the Texas and Pacific Railroad into Sherman, north of Collin County, making the area an important crossroads.[1] In 1868, a military road was cut east to west across Collin County, beginning at Greenville in Hunt County and stretching due west to Fort Richardson, now Jacksboro, Texas. From 1868 until 1873 Fort Richardson was the largest military base in the United States, making Jacksboro a boom town. The size of the military establishment employed to combat the newly aroused Comanche Indians, led by their last warrior chieftain Quanah Parker, insured a constant flow of immigrants and money along this military road. Known as Highway 380 today it connects the Collin County communities of Farmersville, Princeton, McKinney, and Frisco.[2]

In just a little more than car trouble, these two smart young men demonstrate that even on August 23, 1923, roads in Collin County were not always passable.

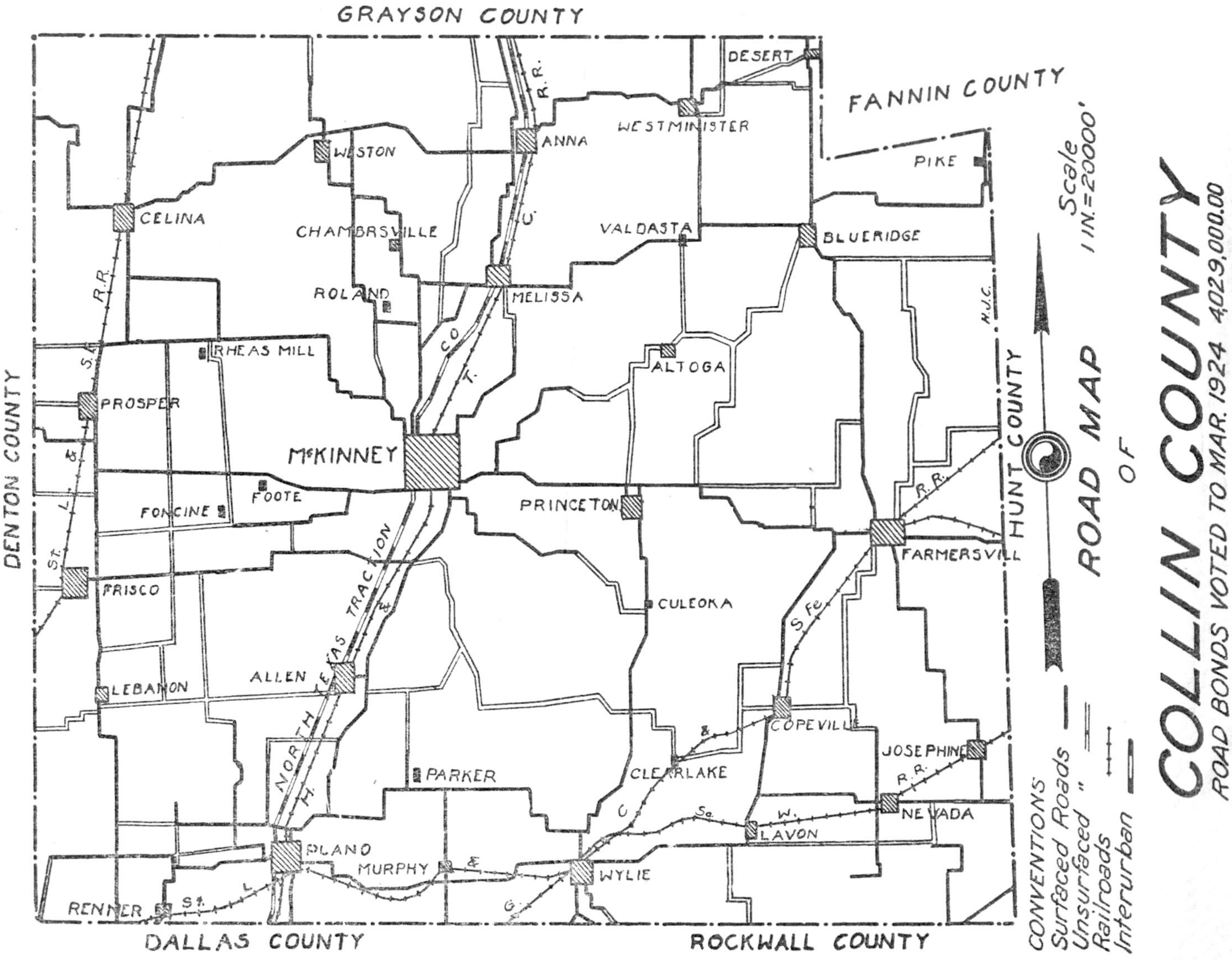

✧

This 1924 map indicates both improved and unimproved (dirt) roads that the county has sold over $4 million in bonds to pay for. With indirect routes and lack of gravel on many roads it is no wonder that the steam railroads and interurban railway became the preferred means of travel. Note that Lake Lavon has yet to be created by the Army Corps of Engineers.

Stagecoach lines used roads that connected Collin County to both Bonham and Dallas. Present-day State Highway 121 was probably the main route connecting Collin County to Bonham, the Civil War headquarters of the Confederate command in Northeast Texas. In the records of the North Texas History Center are original documents relating to the creation of a failed railroad venture proposed by Collin County businessmen after the Civil War. This would-be railroad was charted to follow a route almost identical to present-day Highway 121 into McKinney and Bonham. US Highway 75 has a similar history, as it roughly parallels the old railroad right-of-way of the Southern Pacific, successor to the Houston and Texas Central Railway.

In 1879 a state law was passed requiring that males between the ages of 18 and 45 work at least 10 days a year on maintenance of public roads. It was not until 1899 that the first automobile appeared in Dallas but by 1907 there were enough "horseless carriages" in the state that vehicle registration with the county became a requirement. The speed limit was 18 miles per hour, and the automobile driver was required to always yield to horse-drawn conveyances. Despite the increasing number of vehicles by 1912, only one-fourth of the state's 130,000 miles of road had been graded, and this was accomplished by dragging a log behind a team of mules. Only 5,000 miles of road had any kind of surface upon them, and it was not necessarily pavement.[3]

U. S. Highway 75 was officially designated in 1927 as beginning at the Oklahoma/Texas State Line north of Denison and running through Sherman, Collin County, Dallas, and other cities along the route to Galveston. The Sedalia Trail used by cowboys for driving cattle until 1873, and later known as Preston Road, became State Highway 289 in 1939. State Highway 5 was designated in 1959 as the road connecting Allen, Fairview, McKinney, Melissa, and Anna when the route of U. S. Highway 75 was reestablished further west. In the 1960s the towns of McKinney and Plano could be seen from Highway 75 at some distance to the east of the road; it was not until 1987 that McKinney and Richardson had grown far enough westward to be designated as officially being on the route.[4]

The earliest Collin County Farm-to-Market Roads were designated in 1945 and included FM 544, now a busy thoroughfare in Plano. Paving started in 1946, but most farmers still drove their produce to market over dirt roads. It was not until the passage of the Colson-Briscoe Act of 1949 that the Texas Farm-to-Market Road system saw major expansion and upgrade by paving existing roads and the new construction of others. By 1950 Collin County reaped the benefit of improved rural transportation, becoming one of the most intensely farmed counties in the state. Forty-two thousand bales of cotton were processed in the county during 1946, and by 1950 cotton was the leading crop. The Texas FM system of 1989 included 41,755 miles of pavement, making it the most extensive network of secondary roads in the world.[5]

Planning began in 1962 for the Dallas North Tollway which would eventually reach Collin County. In 1965 a revenue bond issue was successfully underwritten for the Tollway and the first construction contract was awarded the following year. The first stretch was built on the Cotton Belt railroad right of way in Dallas. Opening of this segment occurred on February 11, 1968, with Highway 635 as its northern terminus. The extension into Collin County was studied from 1977 to 1979 and the twelve mile addition northward from Highway 635 to Highway 121 was deemed feasible. Phase I of the extension began in 1983 and was completed in December 1987 to as far north as

Below: Dr. and Mrs. J. T. Mantooth set out on a winter's day in their Model T businessman's coupe.

Bottom: Collin McKinney's home passes the J. B. Wilmeth home on highway 75 (now highway 5) in 1936 on its move from Anna to McKinney for exhibit during the Texas Statehood Centenary. A major improvement over the former dirt track, the blacktop surfaced two lane road was the only way to get to Dallas from the county seat.

✧

In this 1917 photograph Viola Poole McGee is at the wheel of a small touring car as one of the girls from her Collin County Home Demonstration Club crank starts it. Those white dresses are not going to be that way for long.

Briargrove Lane in Dallas. Phase II began construction in 1989, completed and open to traffic to State Highway 121 in 1994. During construction, the Texas Turnpike Authority had agreed to become the first turnpike in the United States to use electronic tolling. The Radio Frequency ID technology utilized in the tolltag system was developed by scientists from Los Alamos National Laboratory, the birthplace of the atomic bomb. The initial tests were not always successful—in one case a windshield-mounted transponder caught fire in a Turnpike employee vehicle while being driven. Eventually tests proved the technology reliable and noted that it was impossible for a vehicle using a tolltag to avoid paying toll by driving too fast.

In 1997 the Texas Turnpike Authority transferred its assets to the new North Texas Tollway Authority (NTTA). The following year Segment I of the George Bush Turnpike opened to traffic between Preston and Midway roads. In 1999, Segment II of the Bush Turnpike was opened. The Dallas North Tollway began extending its reach further north into Collin County in 2005 as construction began on Phase III. This phase was completed and opened to Highway 380 on September 28, 2007. The Phase 4 project began in January 2008 with a public meeting in Prosper. This will take drivers as far north as the Collin/Grayson County line. By fiscal year-end 2008, NTTA recorded 1,231,000 transactions on all of its roads per day, and on September 1, 2008, State Highway 121 officially became part of the NTTA System. Late in 2007 the NTTA provided a $3.2 billion upfront payment to the North Texas region for the right to construct the remaining segments of the 121 Tollway and to maintain and operate the road for fifty years. The money will be used for infrastructure projects throughout the region, and in 2008 the NTTA awarded more work to contractors than ever before.

✧

Left: Looking north on Tennessee Street towards the intersection of Virginia Street, c. 1900, McKinney. The late afternoon sun casts a shadow of the courthouse on the dirt street. Smith Bros. Drug Store existed in at least two locations in this block from 1859 until 2008.

Below: This May 13, 1913, scene of the business district in Weston shows approximately twenty-five early automobiles, mostly Model T Fords. This appears to be a rally, as Weston would never have had this many cars (or people) at the time. One of the cars has a pennant on it indicating it is from Celina. Drivers stand around their cars while women and children are in a group on the right side. The dirt road and one very crooked telephone pole helps establish the time period. On the left is a shoe store and the Stiles General Store.

Right: This view of Parker Road and US75 Intersection taken in February of 1959 shows farmland and little traffic, a far cry from the view today.

PHOTOGRAPH COURTESY OF TXDOT.

Below: A Collin County bridge in 1921.

PHOTOGRAPH COURTESY OF TXDOT.

Opposite, top: Just outside of Plano, 1921 before the road was paved.

PHOTOGRAPH COURTESY OF TXDOT.

Opposite, bottom, left and right: Images from the Federal Aid Notebook of 1921 show a close-up on construction of a bridge. Bridges and roads helped move Collin County forward on the road of progress.

PHOTOGRAPH COURTESY OF TXDOT.

DALLAS 30
FRISCO 11
DENTON 38
FAIRVIEW-GROCERY

✧

Opposite, top: A rural view from the Federal Aid Project notebooks.

PHOTOGRAPH COURTESY OF TXDOT.

Opposite, middle: The Fairview Grocery has a bus parked out front, while the star sign shows the location of gasoline and motor oil. According to the road sign it is 11 miles to Frisco, 30 to Dallas, 38 to Denton or 61 to Waxahachie.

PHOTOGRAPH COURTESY OF TXDOT.

Opposite, bottom: A child stands in the dirt street in this view. A fire hydrant and telephone poles show signs of progress.

PHOTOGRAPH COURTESY OF TXDOT.

Top: Ruts abound on dirt roads in Collin County.

PHOTOGRAPH COURTESY OF TXDOT.

Middle: A view of the roads in McKinney.

PHOTOGRAPH COURTESY OF TXDOT.

Bottom: Texas Highway Department Division 18.

PHOTOGRAPH COURTESY OF TXDOT.

Above: *A view of the courthouse from the southeast corner of the McKinney Square. The statue of Throckmorton can be seen on the northeast corner. This photograph was taken after the renovation in 1927 when the elaborate architecture was simplified.*
PHOTOGRAPH COURTESY OF TXDOT.

Right: Smith's Garage, Celina, Texas, c. 1920. Cars brought with them many complementary businesses: garages, gas stations, tire sales, and more.

CHAPTER VII

AGRICULTURE, COTTON, AND INDUSTRY

Once the railroads, highways and public roads were in place, agricultural production in Collin County entered a boom period that lasted from about 1890 until the Great Depression of the 1930s. As early as 1870, land prices in the county began to rapidly appreciate in anticipation of the coming railroad, but they skyrocketed again during the agricultural boom. Land in Collin County went from $2 to $20 an acre in the 1890s. The greatest increase occurred from 1910 to 1920, when prices rose from $50 to $150 per acre. Due to the high cost of land, by 1920 over sixty-eight percent of the farmers in Collin County were tenant farmers who never owned the land that they farmed.[1]

John Wells inspecting a sweetclover crop in 1965.

✧

Top: Binding and mowing with mule teams at Watkins' farm, c. 1900.

Above: Binding hay near Nevada, Texas, c. 1939.

Below: Working the fields was a part of life in early twentieth century Collin County.

Tenant farming had been in existence since the colonial period in America but statistics on the practice were not kept until 1880. The share tenant, or sharecropping arrangement, was the most common agreement between the tenant farmer—who rented the land—and the landowner. The tenant farmer paid the landowner by sharing a percentage of the harvested crop, and so the tenant farmer worked without pay until that time. Many saw tenant farming as an agricultural ladder that could lead to farm ownership under the right conditions. Soon a hierarchy developed among tenant farmers, with the share tenants supplying mules, seed, and farming supplies while paying the landowner one third of a cotton crop and one fourth of a grain crop. Sharecroppers were at the bottom of the hierarchy, as they supplied their labor but no equipment, seed or supplies and they typically paid the owner one-half of what they grew.[2]

Most of the farm families in Collin County produced a combination of cotton, corn, oats and wheat. The relative amount of the different crops varied with the farmer's estimation of what price the crop would bring at market. Corn production in the county soared from 64,903 acres in 1890 to 145,656 acres in 1910, only to see a reduction to 73,258 acres in 1920. Wheat production peaked during the boom of 1900 at 82,469 acres but fell to 15,082 acres in 1910. By 1900 Collin County was ranked fourteenth in the United States for agricultural production, with 509,419 acres under cultivation—the all-time high. The population of the county had also virtually doubled in the twenty-year period from 1880 to 1900, reaching 50,087, a number not to be surpassed for more than sixty years. In 1912, ninety-five percent of the county was under cultivation. During the boom period, the average size plot was 75 acres per family. Cotton was king in Collin County: in 1860 only 16 bales were produced, but by 1920 that number rose to 49,311 bales produced from 176,901 acres. The estimated dollar value of Collin County farms increased from about $3 million to well over $84 million by 1920. By 1925, 74 percent of the farmers in Collin County were tenant farmers.[3]

Life for most tenant farmers was difficult, as they could not afford the cost of land or livestock and were subject to the whims of Mother Nature and the market economy. Many tenant families lived a semi-nomadic life,

moving from farm to farm at the expiration of each year's tenant contract. Families usually consisted of ten or more members, as women married as early as age fourteen and began having children immediately. Larger families meant less money available for store-bought clothing, so the women of the family made clothes from flour or fertilizer sacks. The occasional store-bought clothing was handed down from child to child and held together with patches. Many families could not afford shoes for their children, so they went barefoot. Healthcare was non-existent, so tenant families depended on home remedies for their illnesses.

The landowners on the other hand, lived a prosperous existence, like Olney Davis, a Plano banker and entrepreneur who owned 2,000 acres of land operated solely with tenant labor. "Gentlemen farmers" like Hunter Farrell owned several businesses including a cotton gin,

✧

Above: A Collin County family of tenant farmers.

Below: This is thought to be the cook shack M. Williams used with his thresher. Williams was a custom thresherman, who took his equipment from one farm to the next. In the background is part of Isaac Grave's house, now the southeast corner of Highways 75 and 380 in McKinney.

producing only a small crop on his lands, most of which were dedicated to producing gravel. Some tenant farmers in Collin County, like John McDonald and Bud Thornton, did eventually save enough money to own automobiles and send their children to college. Walter Barkley, an African-American tenant on the Farrell-Wilson farm, eventually bought his own land. Many tenant farmers enjoyed good relations with the landowning class; Plano landlord John D. Wells made sure his workers were properly fed. Fannie Harrington and the wives of her sons Walter and Robert ministered to tenant families by offering children's clothing and transportation to church. Many tenants established long-lasting relationships in the community through churches; Eddie Stimpson, N. D. Reece, Irene Carter, and Claude Goode were some of those who became permanent residents of the county.[4]

On November 24, 1909, plans were announced in the *McKinney Daily Gazette* for the establishment of the Lone Star Mill Company, a textile mill that was to use only locally grown cotton. The founding force behind the enterprise, which soon changed its name to the Texas Cotton Mill Company, was J. Perry Burrus, wealthy heir to a fortune made in the flour mill and cotton gin businesses in Collin County. His father, W. C. Burrus, had founded the Burrus Flour Mill in the 1870s and had purchased the Farmers and Merchants Roller Mill in 1892 from D. W. Stouffer. The Burrus family business had expanded throughout the state and became one of the largest suppliers of flour in the Southwest.

The Texas Cotton Mill company began operations in McKinney in January of 1911, with a board of directors comprised of McKinney's most wealthy and influential citizens. Among them were William B. Newsome, J. L. White, George Wilcox, J. L. Lovejoy, Louis Alfred Scott, E. W. Kirkpatrick, John H. Ferguson, and Thomas B. Wilson. Corporate officers included J. Perry Burrus, president; Stephen D. Heard, first vice-president and J. P. Crouch, second vice-president. Rare at the time were five women on the board, including businesswomen Mary Elizabeth Boyd and Willie Emma Proctor Marshall who were also initial investors.[5]

Capacity, production, and housing were expanded numerous times in the teens and twenties. In 1924 the mill sold to Clarence R. Miller for \$1.9 million—a nice return on an initial investment of \$225,000. By 1927 the mill complex included the plant, an office building, three warehouses, a water tower, a cooling pond, and a reservoir. The workers were provided with a boarding house, meeting hall, with more than 75 dwellings near the plant. The largest employer in Collin County for several decades, the mill had more than 520 workers and was only one of two mills west of the Mississippi River that produced colored-print cloth. Collin County was prosperous in the 1920s and that wealth was based on farming.[6]

✧

Opposite, top: A long line of horse-drawn wagons transporting bagged grain wind their way towards the Collin County Mill and Elevator Company, c. 1900. The Houston & Texas Central railroad freight dock is in the background. The fence marks Virginia Street in early McKinley.

Opposite, bottom: A family picks cotton in this publicity photograph from a booklet titled Souvenir Letter, McKinney, Texas, *c. 1900.*

Above: Marshall Watkins plows with his horse and mule.

Above: On May 9, 1918, men gather to examine sixteen month old Fairfax, a prime shorthorn owned by cattleman W. E. Smoot.

Below: The wealth of the county is represented in the hundreds of 480-pound bales of cotton that overflow from the Houston & Central Texas Railroad freight dock in McKinney, c. 1900.

The stock market crash of 1929 heralded the beginning of the Great Depression and falling prices for all commodities, including cotton. The living conditions endured by tenant farmers had long been a political issue, and concern was voiced on a national level by President Franklin D. Roosevelt, whose New Deal policies decreased the number of farmers living in tenancy. Other forces, such as the increased mechanization of farms and employment opportunities in Dallas and other locations outside of Collin County, contributed to a drop in the number of farms in the county—from 6,069 farms in 1930 to 4,771 in 1940. Rural electrical cooperatives established in the late 1930s brought improved conditions to isolated farming communities, and on the

✧

Above: An aerial view of Ashburn General Hospital. The hospital was one of the largest employers in McKinney. Highway 380 can be seen at the top of the photograph.

Left: The main building at the Texas Cotton Mill Company, McKinney, 1913.

To-day's
Special
Choice 75¢

whole, Collin County did not suffer as much during the Great Depression as did other places. However, as late as 1940, the county's unemployment rate was nineteen percent. Although the county's population declined from 50,087 in 1900 to 41,692 in 1950, agriculture began to revive due to improvements in soil-conservation practices and advances in wheat production, which increased from 352,229 bushels in 1949 to 1,224,664 bushels in 1959. Wheat had become the county's cash crop, as it once had been during the Civil War, before the cotton boom. By 1960 only thirty-eight percent of the county's farmers were tenant farmers, and on a state-wide basis there were more tractors in Texas than farms.[7]

Agriculture continued to decline through the 1960s and into the following decades, by 1964 Collin County cotton acreage had decreased to 79,935 acres, while wheat acreage increased to 79,546. The county's largest employer into the 1950s, the Texas Textile Mill in McKinney permanently closed its doors in 1969, the victim of the advent of synthetic fibers and a move of denim production to the Texas—Mexico border in 1964.

In the 1970s the golden age of agriculture in Collin County passed and even the Burrus flour mill in McKinney ceased operations. Today less than two percent of the county's population is employed in agriculture. As noted in an article published July 21, 2009, titled, "where the jobs are" Collin County ranked fifteenth nationally, "...thanks to a swift transition from agriculture to high-tech industries."[8]

Opposite, top: Three men and three women stand in the store of George Washington Pool on the south side of the Nevada Square. From the left: two unknown salesgirls, G. W. Pool, Alabama Bryant Pool, Mr. Pool, John Stanford, and an unknown cousin.

Opposite, bottom: Adam Bond's Menswear Store, c. 1910. Hats in this McKinney store were on special for $.75 and military uniforms were on display above the shelves on the right.

Above: Sunshine Biscuits, bread, and canned goods could all be found at Collin County Seed Co. and Cash Grocery at 301 or 222 East Louisiana Street, McKinney, Texas. Owners: G. C. Walters, C. E. Melton, and J. Perry Watson.

Left: Shopping wasn't the only thing to do in downtown McKinney, the Ritz Theater was a popular spot for people of all ages.

CHAPTER VIII

TECHNOLOGY

Collin County residents can explore preservations like the Heard Museum and Sanctuary pictured here.

There is no better illustration of Collin County's leap from agricultural origins to the forefront of technology than the story of Arthur Andrew Collins and Collins Radio Company. Born to a Kingfisher, Oklahoma, farming family on September 9, 1909, Arthur Collins moved to Iowa with his family at an early age. At Cedar Rapids his father started large-scale farming with the objective of grain production at low cost. At age nine Arthur developed a passion for the newest marvel of his age, radio transmission. One of Arthur's Iowa neighbors would later say of him, "We sensed that Arthur was different, but we did not know that he was a genius. When the rest of us were out playing "cowboys and Indians", Arthur was in the house working on his radios." In 1923, at fourteen, Arthur passed the test for a radio license from the Federal Radio Commission. He soon constructed an amateur radio station, and by age fifteen had communicated with other amateur "ham" radio operators across the United States and the world.[1]

Arthur set up shop in the basement of his home in 1931 and produced the first of many thousand amateur radio transmitters; eventually his company would manufacture communications devices on the Blackland Prairie in Texas, but before that could happen he needed his first big break. That break came in 1933 when the company was chosen by Admiral Richard Byrd and CBS to establish radio communications with Byrd's historic expedition to the South Pole. The publicity put his company on the map, and by the late 1930s Collins Radio made equipment for the U. S. Coast Guard and Dallas-based Braniff Airways. With the advent of World War II, orders poured in to Collins Radio and annual sales grew from $722,000 in 1940 to more than $47 million by 1944. The Collins Autotune transmitter was hailed as one of the most wondrous inventions of its day. Sales growth continued to accelerate, particularly in the defense industry.[2]

Collins was urged by the Defense Department to decentralize his manufacturing facilities for security reasons, so in May 1951 he announced plans for an assembly plant in Richardson, Texas. This facility was the seed for the development of the telecommunications corridor of Texas which would eventually become known as "The Silicon Prairie." In addition to manufacture and assembly, the Richardson complex became the center of Collins Radio's research into the uses of microwave transmissions for communications. Company engineers initially studied potential applications of this new technology for the energy and telephone industries, but based on the studies performed at Richardson, Collins management decided to produce some of the first commercially available microwave equipment in 1952. By the spring of 1954 the first prototype was transmitting between Dallas and Irving, Texas. The first of the company's microwave systems was put into commercial operation by the California Interstate Telephone Company in 1955.

Starting in 1956 the Federal Aviation Administration asked Collins to provide remoting systems for what was then the world's largest communications and radar data handling complex. In so doing Collins Radio became the leader in air traffic control technology.

When NASA launched its first space communications satellite in 1960, Collins Radio's Richardson facilities were enlisted in the experiment. They successfully transmitted a message from Richardson to Cedar Rapids, Iowa, by satellite, the first successful two-way voice transmission via satellite. On August 19, 1960, Collins personnel at Richardson achieved another first: the reception of the first photograph transmitted by satellite. By 1962 Collins Radio was installing multiple data acquisition centers at the Goddard Space Flight Center in Maryland. The company's equipment was also aboard the first manned Mercury space capsule launched in 1961, and eight years later astronaut Neil Armstrong spoke the famous words, "That's one small step for man: one giant leap for mankind" from the moon over Collins Radio equipment.

In 1966 Collins Radio diversified into the mainframe computer manufacturing business by introducing the C-8500 system, which combined multi-speed communication with business and

Left and right: With the growth of the population, major and minor league franchises have chosen to make Collin County home.

scientific data computation for on-line, real-time operations. This was said to be the first commercially available fully-integrated communication, computation, and control system with virtually unlimited expansion capacity. Even the *New York Times* took notice in the April 24, 1969, edition, "Collins is in fact so advanced in computer technology that it may be standing on the threshold of a new era." Collins Radio Company, was on the cusp of taking the lead in the fledgling data processing industry. Events beyond the company's control would prevent that from happening.

By the end of the 1960s the United States government had begun the de-escalation of the Vietnam War, and many defense industry contractors like Collins Radio experienced declining revenues. These companies became either bankruptcies, like jet engine maker Rolls-Royce, or takeover targets like Douglas Aircraft, which merged into McDonnell Aircraft. On March 24, 1969, future Dallas billionaire H. Ross Perot announced a hostile takeover of Collins Radio Company. Collins' management publicly rejected the offer and quickly began the search for a white knight merger partner. On June 1, 1971, Collins Radio and North American Rockwell Corporation agreed to terms. Arthur Collins was replaced as president and chairman of the board of the company he had founded, and on January 14, 1972, he resigned from its board of directors. During that time his replacement restructured the company by reducing nine organizational levels to five, with just four operating groups. Two of the four operating groups, Telecommunications and Switching, and International Operations were moved to Dallas/Richardson. Arthur Collins moved his residence to Dallas where he lived until his death in 1987. His dream lives on in the form of Rockwell Collins, a New York Stock Exchange listed company with a market capitalization of $8.7 billion dollars. Today nearly seventy percent of all U. S. and allied military airborne communications are transmitted by the company's systems. By 2007, the top three industries in terms of employment growth in Collin County included the electrical equipment and component manufacturing and wireless telecommunications carriers, reflecting the long-term impact of Collins Radio Corporation on the Silicon Prairie.[3]

The other great innovator that spurred the growth of Collin County's technology base is Texas Instruments Corporation. Eugene McDermott founded its predecessor, Geophysical Service Inc. in 1930 as a provider of seismic data to the energy production industry. During World War II the company provided electronic components to the U. S. Signal Corps and submarine detection equipment to the U.S. Navy. In 1951 the company changed its name to Texas Instruments and began manufacturing germanium resistors and expanded into the rapidly growing field of semiconductor development. They had become the first volume manufacturer of silicon transistors by 1954. This set the stage for the company's role in the development of the world's first silicon chip. Company employee Jack Kilby developed the integrated circuit in 1958, and was eventually awarded one-half the Nobel Prize in Physics in 2000 for that accomplishment. However, it was another Texas Instruments

Above: Kilby receives his Nobel Prize in 2000 from King Carl XVI Gustaf of Sweden.

Below: Though shopping has changed since the days of Woolworth, retail sales are an important economic force in twenty-first century Collin County.

PHOTOGRAPH COURTESY OF ORISON'S ART & FRAMING AND RICK WELLS.

employee, Gary Boone, who received the first patent awarded for a microprocessor in 1971. Under Kilby's direction the company developed the first hand-held electronic calculator in 1967. Initially priced at $150, calculators of like functionality would sell for $3.50 or less, as supply expanded to meet demand. Today the company is considered the leading supplier of digital signal processors and analog devices in the world. In 2009 TI had a market capitalization of $32 billion and was honored as one of the world's most ethical companies for the third year in a row by Ethisphere.[4] Texas Instruments is one of the largest employers in Collin County.

Other high-technology employers in Collin County are later arrivals, such as Electronic Data Systems, now known as EDS, a subsidiary of Hewlett-Packard (HP). Founded in Dallas in 1962 by H. Ross Perot, the firm's first client was Collins Radio Company, which purchased data processing services or "computer time" from Perot's fledgling company. It was through EDS that Perot later sought control of Collins Radio. In the early 1980s EDS signed a federal government contract for data processing services that was the largest deal of its kind at the time. Needing additional space for his operations, Perot purchased 2,700 acres of land in Plano and created Legacy Business Park. In June 1984 General Motors (GM) paid $2.8 billion for EDS and the following year the company moved to its new headquarters in Collin County. Twelve years later GM spun off EDS into a separate company that continued to operate as a provider of information technology outsourcing from its Plano headquarters. On May 13, 2008, EDS and HP signed a definitive agreement for HP to acquire EDS for $13.9 billion. The companies' collective services businesses, as of the end of each company's 2007 fiscal year, had annual revenues of more than $38 billion[5]. At that point the 2007 combined companies had annual revenues in excess of $38 billion. Despite changes in ownership, EDS continues to reside in Plano

Above: Tall Goldenrod.

PHOTO COURTESY OF MICHELLE SCHNEIDER.

Below: Contemporary map of Collin County with select historic ghost towns indicated.

COURTESY OF BRET FENSTER, GIS SERVICES, COLLIN COUNTY.

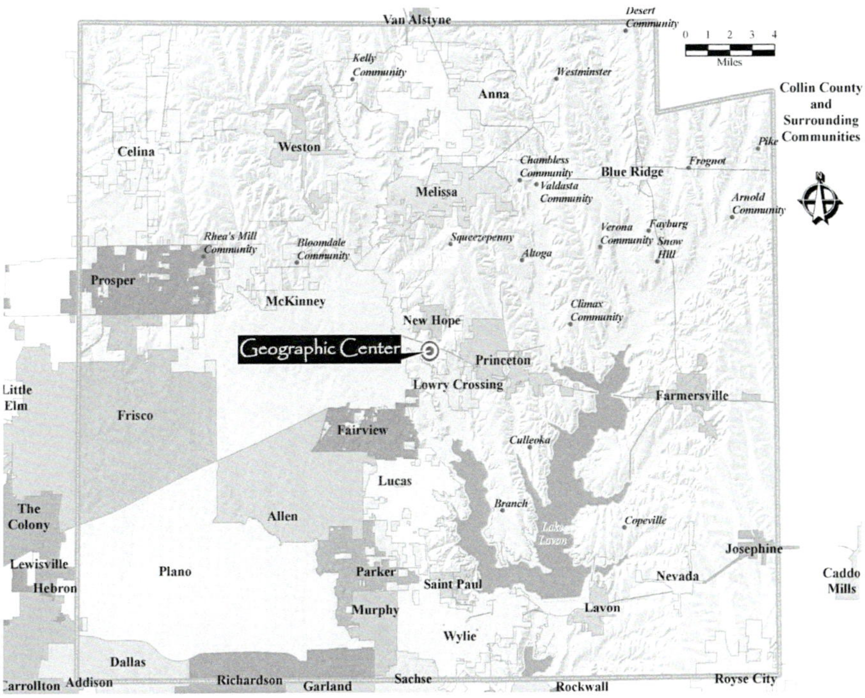

✧

Above: The Central National Bank was instrumental in the financial livelihood of Collin County.

PHOTOGRAPH COURTESY OF ORISON'S ART & FRAMING AND RICK WELLS.

Below: Though technology and progress have dominated the twentieth and early twenty-first centuries, pockets of Collin County are still agricultural.

in the Legacy business park, alongside other corporate giants such as Dr Pepper Snapple, Ericsson, AT&T Wireless, Frito-Lay, JCPenney and many others.[6]

Legacy Business Park is located along what was once the Sedalia/Shawnee Trail. This swath of prairie, like the rest of Collin County, has seen the rise and fall of the cattle industry as well as the vast changes in technology that has allowed for the success of multiple Fortune 500 companies.

Since 2004, Comerica Bank has annually recognized the sixty fastest growing companies in Collin County with its Collin 60 Awards. Many of those recognized are companies like Genband, Inc. A developer of next-generation information processing infrastructure solutions that allow transmission of multimedia services over the Internet, Genband was rated number one in growth out of the top sixty companies in 2009, with sales growing from $4 million in 2004 to over $144 million in 2008.[7]

The growth of technology employment in Collin County shows just how far things have advanced from humble beginnings on the Blackland Prairie. From prehistory to the present, those who settled its fertile ground were by necessity explorers; those who elected to stay were by necessity innovators. Where cattle empires once rose from the trackless Blackland Prairie, corporate empires now chart their course along the track of international trend analysis. From the lignite-fired hearths of the Stone-Age Clovis nomads to the laser-driven semiconductors of the denizens of the Digital Age, a creative energy has propelled the people of Collin County forward and onward into an ever-expanding future.

Bibliography

Chapter I

Benjamin A. Witt, "Differential Use of Space: An Analysis of the Aubrey Clovis Site" Master's Thesis, UNT.

David La Vere, *Life Among the Texas Indians.*

F. Todd Smith, *The Caddo Indians.*

Handbook of Texas Online.

North Texas Tollway Authority, "Archeological Dig Unearths Ancient Treasures" *Driving Forward.*

Timothy K. Perttula, *The prehistory of Texas.*

Endnotes

Chapter I

1. F. Todd Smith, *The Caddo Indians* (College Station: Texas A&M University Press, 1995).

Chapter II

1. Harold Beam, "A History of Collin County, Texas". Master's Thesis, University of Texas, 1951.
2. The McDonald cabin is, of this date, the only known remaining cabin of the Peters Colony. The log cabin itself is still intact inside the walls of the former Ben and Orene Pitts residence on James Pitts Road. A Collin County Historical Marker was placed there.
3. Today, the site of the Muncey family massacre is commemorated by a Texas Historical Commission marker on the Spring Creek Parkway campus of Collin County Community College.
4. Friends of the Plano Public Library, *Plano, Texas: The Early Years.* (Wolfe City, Henington Pub. Co., 1985) p. 71.
5. Harold Beam, "A History of Collin County, Texas". Master's Thesis, University of Texas, Austin, p. 37.
6. Friends of the Plano Library, *Plano, Texas: The Early Years,* p. 79.
7. Coit Family Papers, Dallas Historical Society, Dallas, Texas. The Dallas Historical Society generously temporarily loaned the Coit Papers to the North Texas History Center. Over 800 pages of this collection have been digitized by the North Texas History Center for future research and exhibit.
8. Clark, James Lemuel, *Civil War Recollections of James Lemuel Clark.* (College Station, Texas A&M University Press, 1984.) p. 104.

Chapter III

1. Petersen, Paul R. *Quantrill in Texas.* (Nashville, Cumberland House, 2007.) p. 146.
2. *Handbook of Texas Online,* s. v., "William Clarke Quantrill," http://www.tshaonline.org/handbook/online/articles/QQ/fqu3.html (accessed December 6, 2009).
3. Thomas Caute Reynolds Collection, Library of Congress, Washington, D. C.

Chapter IV

1. Originally known as Rhea's Mills, the name was changed to Rhea Mills in 1892
2. Wayne Gard, "The Shawnee Trail" *Southwestern Historical Quarterly*, Vol. LVI No. 3 (January, 1953) p. 363.
3. Murrah, David J. C. C. *Slaughter, rancher, banker, Baptist.* (Austin, University of Texas Press, 1981) pp. 18-19.
4. The Correspondence of Henrietta Mercer Chiles Knight. Kansas State Historical Society, Topeka, Kansas.
5. H. M. Parvin to G. M. Slaughter, 16 January 1869. North Texas History Center, McKinney, Texas.
6. *Weekly State Journal*, December 1, 1870.
7. Davis Hester to S. J. Hester, 4 May 1870. Adeline Bowling Letters, Special Collections, Duke University, Durham, North Carolina.
8. Holden, William Curry. *Rollie Burns, or, An account of the ranching industry on the south Plains.* (College Station, Texas A&M University Press, 1986) pp.30-44. J. A. Rickard, "The cattle ranch industry of the Texas South Plains", Master's Thesis, University of Texas, Austin, 1927.
9. Spellman, Paul N. *Captain J. A. Brooks: Texas Ranger.* (Denton, University of North Texas Press, 2007) p. 19.

Chapter V

1. Davis Hester to S. J. Hester, 4 May 1870. Adeline Bowling Letters, Special Collections, Duke University.
2. Smallwood, James M., *Murder and Mayhem; the War of Reconstruction in Texas.* (College Station, Texas A&M University, 2003). pp. 100, 110. Harold Beam, "A History of Collin County, Texas" Master's Thesis, University of Texas,. August, 1951. *McKinney Messenger,* October 21, 1871.
3. Reed, S. G. *A History of the Texas Railroads....* (Houston, St. Clair Publishing Co., 1941) p. 210. *Handbook of Texas Online,* s. v. "Collin County," http://www.tshaonline.org/handbook/online/articles/CC/hcc16.html (accessed August 8, 2009). Bryan Lean, "Technology That Changed North Texas", North Texas History Center, McKinney, Texas, 2007. *McKinney Weekly Enquirer*, January 5, 1878. Moneyhon, Carl H. *Texas after the Civil War.* (College Station, Texas A&M University, 2004.) p 161. *Dallas Herald,* January 20, 1877.
4. *McKinney Weekly Enquirer*, January 5, 1878. *Dallas Herald,* August 4, 1877. 1880 Census data for Collin County, Texas.
5. Harold Beam, "A History of Collin County", op cit.
6. "Historic Markers of Grayson County", Grayson County Historical Society, Sherman, Texas, 1996. *Handbook of Texas Online,* s. v. "Texas Electric Railway," http://www.tshaonline.org/handbook/online/articles/TT/eqt13.html (accessed October 19, 2009).
7. *Dallas Area Rapid Transit*, "DART History," http://www.dart.org/about/history.asp (accessed on October 19, 2009).

Chapter VI

1. *Handbook of Texas Online*, s. v. "Central National Road," http://www.tshaonline.org/handbook/online/articles/CC/erc1.html (accessed November 7, 2009). George Pearis Brown, The Brown Papers, North Texas History Center.
2. Dr. David F. Kirkpatrick, "Memoirs of Southeast Denton County," http://mikecochran.net/Dr.Kirkpatrick_Memoirs.html (accessed May 13, 2009). McConnell, H. H. *Five years a cavalryman; or, sketches of regular army life on the Texas frontier, twenty odd years ago.* (Jacksboro, J. N. Rogers & Co., 1889) pp. 159-162. Strong, Henry W. *My frontier days & Indian fights on the plains of Texas.* (Self-published, 1926) p. 30.
3. Meyer, Judy. *A History of the North Texas Tollway Authority.* (Dallas, North Texas Tollway Authority, 2003) pp 3-4. *Handbook of Texas Online,* s. v. "Highway Development," http://www.tshaonline.org/handbook/online/articles/HH/erh2.html (accessed September 23, 2009).
4. *Texas Department of Transportation Highway Designation File,* s. v. "U. S. highway No. 75," and "State Highway No. 5," http://www.dot.state.tx.us/tpp/hwy/sh/sh0005.htm. (accessed November 7, 2009).
5. *Handbook of Texas Online,* s. v. "Highway Development," op cit. Harold Beam, "A History of Collin County, Texas", Masters Thesis, University of Texas, 1951. *Texas Department of Transportation Highway Designation File,* s. v., "State Highway No. 289," http://www.dot.state.tx.us/tpp/hwy/sh/sh0289.htm (accessed November 7, 2009).

Chapter VII

1. Brown, Heather. *Tenant Farming in Collin County,* 1890-1920. (Plano, Heritage Farmstead Association, 1997).
2. *Handbook of Texas Online*, s. v. "Farm Tenancy," http://www.tshaonline.org/handbook/online/articles/FF/aefmu.html (accessed October 18, 2009).
3. Brown, Tenant Farming, op cit. *Handbook of Texas Online*, s. v. "Collin County," http://www.tshaonline.org/handbook/online/articles/CC/hcc16.html (accessed August 8, 2009).
4. Brown, *Tenant Farming*, op cit.
5. Interweaving History: The Texas Textile Mill and McKinney, Texas, 1903–1968, Thesis, Deborah Kilgore
6. "McKinney Cotton Mill Historic District" file, North Texas History Center.
7. *Handbook of Texas Online*, s. v. "Collin County," "Farm Tenancy," op cit.
8. "Soil Survey, Collin County, Texas" United States Department of Agriculture, June 1969. McKinney Cotton Mill Historic District file, op cit. Brown, *Tenant Farming,* op cit. *CNNMoney.com*, s. v. "Where the jobs are," http://www.cnnmoney.com. (accessed November 22, 2009).

Chapter VIII

1. Braband, Ken C. *The first 50 years: a history of Collins Radio Company and the Collins Division of Rockwell International.* (Cedar Rapids, Rockwell International, 1983)pp. 1-4.
2. "C. R.'s Collins Radio took radio to new heights," *Cedar Rapids Gazette,* August 8, 1999.
3. Ibid. Braband, *The First 50 Years,* pp. 95-96, 105-106, 127-129, 162-178. *Rockwell Collins, Inc.*, s. v., "Rockwell Collins History," http://www.rockwellcollins.com/about/history/prn_index.html. (accessed on January 4, 2010).
4. Reid, T. R. *The Chip: How Two Americans Invented the Microchip and Launched a Revolution.* (New York, Random House, 2001) pp. 62-74, 177, 249-56. *Ethisphere*, s. v., "2009 World's Most Ethical Companies," http://ethisphere.com/wme2009. (accessed on January 14, 2010). *ValueLine Investment Survey*, s. v., "Texas Instruments," http://www.valueline.com. (accessed on January 8, 2010).
5. HP News Release, "HP to Acquire EDS for $13.9 Billion", http://www.hp.com/hpinfo/newsroom/press/2008/080513a.html. (accessed on July 28, 2010).
6. *Plano Economic Development Board*, s. v., "The Plano Story," and "Legacy," http://www.planotexas.org/The-Plano-Story.aspx. (accessed on January 17, 2010). *Hewlett Packard*, s. v., "HP to Acquire EDS for $13.9 Billion," http//www.hp.com/hpinfo/newsroom/press/2008/080513a.html. (accessed on January 17, 2010).
7. *Reuters*, " s. v., "GENBAND Named Fastest Growing Company in the Area by Comerica Bank Collin 60 Program," http://www.reuters.com/articlePrint?articleId=US136480%2B07-May-2009%2BBW20090507. (accessed on November 22, 2009).

Sharing the Heritage

Historic profiles of businesses, organizations, and families that have contributed to the development and economic base of Collin County

ENCORE WIRE CORPORATION

Since its inception in 1989, Encore Wire has called McKinney, Texas, home. Born as a small residential wire manufacturer, Encore Wire Corporation is now a billion-dollar, publicly traded company manufacturing commercial and residential building wire, as well as Metal-Clad and Armor-Clad cable, which was introduced in 2006. The company's corporate headquarters and manufacturing facilities are strategically located on a single, 182 acre campus. By combining management offices and state-of-the-art manufacturing facilities, Encore is able to deliver unmatched customer value by maintaining strict control of all aspects of the business.

Now a leader in low-cost manufacturing of copper electrical building wire and cable, Encore Wire is a major supplier of both residential wire for interior electrical wiring in homes, apartments and manufactured housing, and commercial wire for electrical distribution in commercial and industrial buildings.

Vincent A. Rego and Donald M. Spurgin founded Encore in 1989. The cofounders, who had been colleagues in the wire and cable business since the mid-1950s, were formally principal executive officers of Capital Wire and Cable Corporation until the sale of that company to The Penn Central Corporation in 1988.

Cofounder and chairman Rego, a native of Rhode Island, first came to Texas with his wife, Dorothy, in 1953 after moving to a new wire plant in Plano. He quickly found his niche in the trade and never tired of seeing his dreams become a reality. Soon recognized as an innovative leader and outstanding force within the wire industry he and his team bought and sold a wire company in the area before setting their sights upon a "rundown mobile home plant" about thirty-five miles north of Dallas on ten acres in McKinney. Regos' team bought the site, with a truck well and shipping dock, and formed Encore Wire in 1989. The company began operations in February of 1990 and, through plant expansions in March of 1991 and January of 1992, tripled its original production capacity and increased its net sales from $10.7 million in 1990 to $31 million in 1991.

Encore quickly found its pace in the technology race and made its first public offering on July 16, 1992. By 1994 sales had climbed to over $100 million and the company, which had strictly offered residential wire as a short-line producer, was approved for a $15-million expansion into a second plant. Now a full-line producer, the company quickly set the standard for innovation, customer service, and high quality within the competitive industry. Sales reached to over $1 billion in 2006 and its facilities today include over 750 employees and 1.4 million square feet on 182 acres.

Electrical contractors and distributors from around the country have come to appreciate one of Encore's most important innovations in the wire industry—color-coated, commercial feeder wire. The colored wire ensures that electrical contractors install commercial wire safely and efficiently in accordance with National Electrical Codes. High visibility labeling also allows the consumer to easily identify wire types and sizes at a glance, from any angle.

Encore is in the forefront of the development and construction of equipment that enables the company to manage every stage of wire manufacturing—from production, warehousing, shipping, to support processes.

✧

Aerial view of Encore's facilities.

As Encore has grown to become one of the most successful businesses of its kind in the nation, it continues to set a high mark in meeting the demands of distributors with uniquely quick shipping and delivery capabilities. The company emphasizes personal responsibility and accuracy in order and packing procedures, while they consistently maintain an exceptional ninety-nine percent plus order fill rate and therefore create fewer backorders and minimize operational problems and administrative costs.

Since its creation, Encore Wire Corporation has built its success with a firm focus on customer service. A philosophy of "select service" remains Encore's standard for success. The company continues to offer one-stop sourcing for residential and commercial building wire needs. Inventory levels remain "broad and deep" and characterize a well established, strong customer loyalty, rapidly handling customer inquiries, orders, and shipments.

Encore is publicly traded on the NASDAQ market as "WIRE" and has been recognized throughout the industry with numerous product and service awards, including Showstopper Awards for the National Electrical Contractors' Association (NECA) in 2001 as well as the EC&M and CEE News Electrical Product of the Year in 2002.

In November of 2004, Encore Wire received awards for "Supplier of the Year" and "Excellence in Service and Delivery" and received the 2006 "Excellence in Service and Support" all from the IMARK Group, a large national marketing group of electrical distributors in which members rate all suppliers' performances. Border States Electric named Encore as Vendor of the Year for Service Excellence in both 2006 and 2009, and received the Independent Electric's Supplier of the Year award in 2008 and The Reynolds Company's Vendor of the Year award in 2009.

Before Rego's passing in 2009, he commented on his company's outstanding success, "There is no substitute for setting high goals and working hard every day to achieve them. Our staff is dedicated to being the best supplier in the electrical industry by exceeding customer expectations. We will continue to focus on these important criteria in addition to innovating new wire products and maintaining strong personal relationships with our valued customers as we continue to grow Encore Wire in the future."

It is indeed a bright future for Encore as it continues to grow the company with innovative services and focuses on customer relations and efficient and low cost products to maintain profitability. By further expanding its share of the markets for building wire, Encore remains focused upon emphasizing a high level of customer service and low cost production, as well as the addition of new products that compliment its current production.

Encore Wire has built its historic reputation as being the industry leader in service delivery exceeding customer expectations. Building solid relationships with a select family of loyal customers has driven the company's growth and ensures its future success, for Encore customers know that a handshake seals a deal and its word means more than a written contract. Its dedicated employees remain driven by old-fashioned values and a disciplined focus on maintaining those values with every customer and across the communities they serve. McKinney, Texas, is a remarkable community and has been a major contributing factor for Encore Wire Corporation's continued success for over twenty years.

President and Chief Executive Officer Daniel L. Jones believes that Encore Wire's unwavering strategy for success—customer service, product innovation, low-cost production, and efficient plant design—are key to the effective partnerships it has garnered all across the industry for over two decades. "We will continue our efforts to grow Encore organically by providing our customers industry-leading order fill rates and innovative products...we are grateful to our stockholders for their support and wish to recognize the ongoing devotion and hard work of all our employees and associates whose efforts result in our continued growth and success."

For more information about Encore, visit the company online at www.encorewire.com.

City of McKinney

The elements that established McKinney as unique from its very beginnings are the same that continue to attract residents, visitors and businesses to the community today. Beautiful tree-lined streets, diverse residential neighborhoods, outstanding educational opportunities, a robust business environment, a charming, historic downtown and a strong sense of community make McKinney truly stand out.

The Unique by nature℠ brand so strongly associated with the city is more than a tagline, it is a commitment that embodies the community's willingness to work together to make McKinney a great place to be. As one of the fastest-growing cities in the nation, residents, businesses and visitors alike show that they strongly embrace the community's vision and strong overall quality of life.

Just thirty miles north of downtown Dallas, McKinney is a picturesque city with a small-town feel that is quite different from the Metroplex's urban sprawl. Its friendly charm, green spaces and comfortable pace belie the fact that McKinney, with a population of nearly 128,000, is one of the ten fastest-growing cities in America.

The nation continues to recognize McKinney as a stand-out community with some of the most recent accolades including the August 2010 issue of *Money Magazine* ranking McKinney fifth on their list of "Best Places to Live In the Country." Factors considered included employment, schools, crime and safety, as well as overall quality of life aspects including a feeling of community pride. According to the listing, McKinney's historic downtown and hometown spirit set the city apart from the rest of suburban America. "Lots of towns near Dallas have low crime, affordable homes, and good jobs; McKinney is no exception. What makes it stand out is its gem of a downtown...Though McKinney has grown like mad over the past decade, you'd never suspect it when driving through its tree-filled communities surrounded by ponds, parks, and hiking trails." *Money Magazine*.

The city's downtown square offers more than 120 unique shops and more than a dozen exceptional restaurants, including upscale restaurants featuring award-winning chefs, sandwich and coffee shops, outdoor patio dining and neighborhood pubs. If shopping is your thing, downtown McKinney offers an assortment of specialty shops, art galleries featuring the works of local artists, furniture stores, exquisite antique collections, gift shops and apparel boutiques. Thousands of people flock to downtown for annual events such as Oktoberfest, Dickens of a Christmas and Bike the Bricks.

The original Collin County Courthouse stands at the center of McKinney's historic downtown square. Reborn in 2006 as the McKinney Performing Arts Center (MPAC), the performing arts venue features a 480-seat theater suitable for intimate arts performances, lectures and events. In addition to the theater, MPAC includes several multipurpose spaces, including a reception hall, auditorium, rehearsal space, audiovisual-equipped classrooms, art gallery and executive suites.

The spotlight shines bright on McKinney, listing the city as one of the best places to be in many polls. McKinney was named one of the "25 Best Places to Move" in the country by Forbes.com, as well as making an appearance in many rankings lately: safest cities in the state and country, fastest growing cities in the country, best places to raise a family. McKinney was named one of the 100 best places to raise a family in the country by *BestLife* magazine. The editors of the magazine considered categories like low crime, exceptional schools, strong job market and arts and culture.

McKinney's diverse economy includes a healthy mix of retail, office and manufacturing. Some of McKinney's leading employers include Raytheon, Lattimor Materials, Encore Wire, McKinney Medical Center, United American Insurance, Timber Blind Manufacturing, Orthofix and Simpson Strong-Tie. Businesses with operations in McKinney have led the environmentally sustainable development movement by building offices using green building techniques and meeting stringent platinum standards for Leadership in Energy and Environmental Design (LEED) Certification. McKinney is home to one of the nation's two green Walmart Supercenters as well as the Pat Lobb Toyota dealership—the first automotive dealership in the nation to earn LEED certification.

Collin County Regional Airport is rapidly emerging as the new corporate airport of choice for businesses operating in the North Dallas area. The airport is currently home to several corporate tenants, including Texas Instruments, Hewlett Packard, Crossmark, Inc., Encore Wire, United American Insurance, McKinney Aerospace, Lattimore Materials, Pinjet Aviation and North Dallas Aviation. Collin County Regional Airport is located between SH 121, U.S. 75 and SH 380 and is minutes from downtown Dallas, Richardson's Telecom Corridor and the Millennium and Legacy Business Parks.

Outstanding educational opportunities in McKinney attract residents and help turn out a well-educated workforce for businesses. McKinney Independent School District (MISD) has a strong reputation for academic excellence and for developing well-rounded students. The district is one of the fastest-growing public school districts in Texas and currently enrolls over 24,000 students. Collin College offers degree programs of every level, even doctoral programs, thanks to a new Higher Education Center and a renovated Central Park Campus, the college's first location.

While many factors combine to make McKinney a truly special place in America, it is the people in McKinney who bring these vibrant qualities to life. That community spirit is embodied in a friendly, safe and inviting city that holds strong ties to its roots and history while enjoying rapid economic development and continually adding new amenities that compliment and expand our unique quality of life.

This is McKinney, Texas—Unique by nature.SM

COLLIN COLLEGE

On April 6, 1985, Collin County voters overwhelmingly voted Collin College into existence. The college held its first classes at night on September 3, 1985 at area high schools. The first campus, Central Park Campus, opened in McKinney in January 1986. The first graduation ceremony was held May 16, 1987 and was comprised of twelve students. Collin College now offers more than 100 degree and certificate programs and serves more than 51,000 credit and continuing education students annually. The district has seven locations in Allen, Frisco, Plano, McKinney, and Rockwall.

Historically, Collin College is known as a college with preeminent faculty who are noted authors, scholars, patent holders and scientists. Three Collin College professors were named U.S. Professor of the Year within nine years, a highly coveted distinction presented by the Council for Advancement and Support of Education (CASE) and the Carnegie Foundation for the Advancement of Teaching. The college also boasts a Texas Professor of the Year, five Minnie Stevens Piper Professors and two Fulbright scholars.

Collin College has always been a college of firsts. The only public college in the county, Collin College was the first community college in the nation to offer alternative teacher certification and was one of ten in the nation to receive a "Teaching By Choice" award from the American Association of Community Colleges. Collin College was the first Texas community college to offer a pre-admission program, which allows students to earn credit at Collin College and ten major universities simultaneously. The college houses a first-of-its-kind Convergence Technology Center and was named one of sixteen institutions across the nation to watch for civic endeavors by the Case Foundation. Collin College was one of twelve community colleges nationwide to be honored with the Community Engagement Classification by the Carnegie Foundation for the Advancement of Teaching and is the recipient of the national Bellwether Award for innovative practices.

For more than twenty-five years, area residents have benefitted from Collin College's offerings. The college set a new standard of collaboration when it opened the Collin Higher Education Center in 2010. The campus is a university center which offers residents the opportunity to pursue bachelor's, master's and doctoral programs from top area universities.

Collin College will continue to transform the collegiate experience through programs such as

Above: The first Collin College graduation occurred in 1987.

Below: The Collin College Mace, featuring the core values, marks the beginning of graduation.

COLLIN COLLEGE CORE VALUES

We have a passion for:

- Learning
- Service and Involvement
- Creativity and Innovation
- Academic Excellence
- Dignity and Respect
- Integrity

Collin College Mission Statement

Collin College is a student and community-centered institution committed to developing skills, strengthening character, and challenging the intellect.

Above: *The Collin College nursing program began in 1990.*

Weekend College, which offers students the opportunity to earn a degree by taking classes exclusively on the weekends. Collin College offers a Student Leadership Academy, an Honors Institute, eCollege with hundreds of online classes, and a dual credit program, which annually enables hundreds of high school students to earn college credit. Collin College students flourish in the Center for Scholarly and Civic Engagement and the Center for Advanced Studies in Mathematics and Natural Sciences, which offers hands-on undergraduate research experience. At Collin College, it is commonplace for students to have the opportunity to learn from nationally renowned speakers, such as the late Peter Jennings, anchor of ABC's *World News Tonight*, ambassador of the Fulbright Scholars Program Harriet Fulbright and Norman Borlaug, the late Nobel Peace Prize winner.

The heart of Collin College is its students who win national awards, publish their work in national gene banks and international journals and discover asteroids while they earn associate degrees. Within a six-year period, three Collin College students were named to the All-USA Phi Theta Kappa Academic Team. In addition, numerous student organizations have garnered national awards.

Collin College graduates and former students have attended Ivy League and nationally renowned universities such as Yale, Columbia, Cornell, Harvard, and MIT. Their work can be viewed on Broadway, in *TIME*, *Newsweek*, and *Forbes*. Collin College alumni are currently working on cures for cancer, Alzheimer's and numerous diseases plaguing the world. They are nationally acclaimed scientists, actors and artists. The legacy of Collin College—its students—will continue to provide a significant impact, carrying this institution's mission and core values throughout the world.

Below: *The college's university center, Collin Higher Education Center, opened in McKinney in 2010.*

Grayson-Collin Electric Cooperative, Inc.

Grayson-Collin Electric Cooperative, Inc. provides electric energy through a distribution system covering much of Collin and Grayson Counties and portions of Denton, Cooke and Fannin Counties. For much of the history of the Cooperative, the majority of the service area was rural, but the sprawl of the DFW Metroplex has brought increasingly urban characteristics as the suburb communities continue to develop and grow.

In 1935, Congress passed the Rural Electrification Act that created the Rural Electrification Administration under the United States Department of Agriculture. The Act allowed for government guaranteed loans to electric companies to construct electric power lines to the rural areas of the United States.

In September of 1937, after several attempts to loan monies to "traditional" power companies proved unsuccessful, the REA and the legislators who had supported the Act decided to allow farmers, ranchers and local business owners to form not-for-profit electric cooperatives to bring power to the farms.

According to a newsletter produced and mailed in member billing statements in 1958 or 1959, "It was the spring of 1936 when the farmers of this area began to talk about rural electrification and to most of them it seemed like just a dream, but the late J. Thomas Robinson (father of our President, Lewis Robinson) had a different idea; and he was trying to do something about it. He came to G. V. Bray and asked for help in getting the farmers of the area together for a meeting to discuss the possibilities of electrifying their farms. Bray, being well known as a businessman and farmer, helped Robinson, and they finally arranged a meeting, which was held up over the First State Bank in Celina sometime during the summer of 1936. From that meeting, groups began working in different localities and then on September 29, 1937, the first official meeting of the incorporators and directors of the Grayson-Collin Electric Cooperative, Inc., was held at 1:00 p.m. in Van Alstyne. Mr. Bray acted as Chairman of the meeting and was elected president of the Cooperative at the next meeting.

A person had to be a good salesman to sell a farmer on electricity at that time, but after much hard work a contract was let for 105 miles of line, to serve some 300 members, and thus the Cooperative was started."

Farm families paid a five dollar membership fee and committed to purchasing electricity from the Cooperative when the power lines were constructed and energized. With this being the height of the Great Depression, five dollars was a considerable burden for most families; however, the need and desire for electrification outweighed the sacrifice.

The name Rayburn Country Electric Cooperative, Inc., honored Sam Rayburn, a tireless worker on behalf of the "average man" and a moving force behind the Rural Electrification Act.

The outbreak of World War II momentarily halted construction throughout the country in almost all industries, as every effort was put toward supporting the military. There was no metal available to produce the wire that would be strung on the poles that had been placed before the war. In some cases, the poles stood "naked" until the end of the war.

With the end of the war, Grayson-Collin saw an unprecedented growth that would continue through the 1950s and 1960s until congressional members decided that there was no longer a need for the REA. An effort was made to discontinue the funding of the program, with supporters of the movement stating that co-ops had done their job, and the countryside had been electrified. This effort failed and the REA continues to loan money to some electric cooperatives today as the Rural Utility Service or RUS. Through the RUS, money is now lent to electric co-ops, telephone co-ops, and rural water districts. Grayson-Collin Electric Cooperative repaid all of its REA/RUS loans in 1997 and now obtains private financing for construction funds.

Grayson-Collin Electric Cooperative has been based in Van Alstyne, the center of the service area, since 1937. It was initially located on Marshall Street in the downtown square, and today remains at 1096 North Waco Street (State Highway 5). The initial structure was constructed in 1948, while additions have been made several times including a two story office connected to the original building in 2001.

The first street address for Rayburn Country Electric Cooperative, Inc., was the Kaufman County Electric Cooperative, Inc., office building in Kaufman. This remained the business address until June 1, 1986, when Rayburn hired its first staff, a president and administrative assistant, and relocated to Rockwall.

Today, the historic Cooperative continues to meet the challenges of expansion and the ever-changing electric distribution industry, as well as the ever expanding Dallas/Fort Worth Metroplex. In order to accommodate this massive growth in businesses, homes and school districts, its leaders continually search for methods of lowering costs without sacrificing reliability.

As the group moves further into the twenty-first century, people are more attuned to their needs and desires. Instead of just feeling "lucky" to have the REA and its electric co-ops, people now want more information. In that light, *Texas Co-op Power* is published to inform and educate. They are also developing and refining policies and procedures that allow for the interconnection of Distributive Generation for windmills and solar panels and, in 2010, have installed nearly twenty such generators at member residences.

Grayson-Collin Electric Cooperative currently employs more than ninety people, making it one of the largest employers in Van Alstyne. The employees are very active in their communities with many serving in their churches and volunteering as coaches, commissioners or umpires for local youth sports teams. Many are active in civic organizations such as Chambers of Commerce, Rotary Club and the Masonic Lodge, while others serve as members of their city council or school board.

The service area of Grayson-Collin Electric Cooperative contains nineteen public school districts and at least two private schools. Since 1997, they have provided a scholarship to one graduating senior from each of these districts and have provided book covers to students for more than fifty years.

For more information about Collin County's historic electric cooperative, visit them online at www.grayson-collin.coop.

Turrentine-Jackson-Morrow Funeral Directors

Turrentine-Jackson-Morrow is the continuation of a very old business in McKinney.

In 1888, S. J. Massie opened a livery stable business in McKinney dealing in harness and vehicles. From the sale of coffins and rental of wagons to be used as hearses, the livery stable evolved into the S. J. Massie Undertaking Company in 1913. It was located just off the square at 227 East Louisiana Street. It is said that it is the oldest resident funeral home in North Texas.

On October 3, 1941, Massie started the Massie Funeral Home Burial Insurance Association. On May 1, 1945, Audie and Josephine Turrentine and Grady and Mable Jackson purchased the Massie Funeral Home and the Massie Funeral Home Burial Insurance Association.

The business also included an emergency ambulance service. The business was located on the southeast corner of Tennessee and Davis Streets.

The Turrentines and Jacksons worked hard in their business and became very active in McKinney in their church and service organizations with Audie Turrentine serving as president of the McKinney Chamber of Commerce in 1957.

In 1953 the name of the firms were changed to Turrentine-Jackson Mortuary and Turrentine-Jackson Insurance Association. In 1955 the business moved next door (one lot to the south) into a colonial style building. There were two apartments upstairs in the funeral home and Billy Wayne and Annette Turrentine lived in one of them with their children until 1968.

After many years of working in the emergency ambulance business with stories that include getting people to the hospital that had been in accidents, delivering babies, being called to a home to get a person out of the bath tub that was stuck in the tub, and hospital transfers, the emergency ambulance business was sold to the City of McKinney in 1968 for $1.

In 1966 the families purchased Ridgeview Memorial Park located on Highway 75 at Ridgeview Drive. In 1973 the business moved from downtown McKinney to the present-day location at Ridgeview Memorial Park. With this move in 1973 the name of the firm was changed to Turrentine-Jackson-Morrow Funeral Directors. Doyle and Beverly Morrow, the son-in-law and daughter of Grady and Mable Jackson, had been associated with the firm since 1960.

Moving the funeral home to the memorial park location created one of the only family owned full-service funeral facilities in North Texas. The business now includes funeral homes in McKinney/Allen, Frisco, Celina, Gunter, Leonard and Whitewright; memorial parks in McKinney/Allen, Frisco, and Greenville; Collin County's only crematory; T-J-M Life Insurance Company; and two full-service florists—Ridgeview Florist and A Twist Of Lime Floral Design.

In 1945 the company had 7 employees, including family members. Today the business has grown to 84 employees with 9 family members actively working in the business and it is one of the largest family-owned funeral firms in the state.

Opposite, top: S. J. Massey Undertaking Company hearses in 1913.

Opposite, bottom: The Turrentine-Jackson ambulances, c. the 1960s.

Above: The Turrentine-Jackson-Morrow location in McKinney/Allen.

Below: Ridgeview Memorial Park.

Dallas Area Rapid Transit

Dallas Area Rapid Transit gets you around Dallas and twelve surrounding cities with modern public transit services and customer facilities tailored to make your trip fast, comfortable and economical. DART's extensive network of DART Rail, Trinity Railway Express (TRE) and bus services efficiently transports passengers across a 700 square mile service area. DART also operates a system of high occupancy vehicle (HOV) lanes that allows commuters to whiz past freeway traffic jams each weekday.

DART connects you to great work and play destinations in Collin County and beyond. Along the Red Line, you will find places of employment like Cisco, Fujitsu, Rockwell and Texas Instruments Spring Creek Campus; educational institutions such as the University of Texas at Dallas and Collin County Community College (Spring Creek Campus); civic buildings such as the Collin County Sub-Courthouse, Plano City Hall and the Plano Municipal Court; residences such as Eastside Village Apartments and the 15th Street Village Townhomes and Condos; and fun destinations like Historic Downtown Plano, Collin Creek Mall, Haggard Park, the Interurban Railway Station Museum, the Courtyard Theater, ArtCentre of Plano, Eisenbergs SkatePark and Georgia's Farmers Market.

The DART Rail System provides convenient and quick service to destinations in Carrollton, Dallas, Farmers Branch, Garland, Plano and Richardson. Plus, the TRE commuter line links DART customers to Dallas-Fort Worth International Airport and downtown Fort Worth. Free parking is available at most rail stations, and all are served by DART bus routes specially timed to make transfers between buses and trains quick and easy.

DART completed the twenty-eight mile, $1.8 billion Green Line in December 2010, bringing rail service as far south as Pleasant Grove and as far northwest as the cities of Farmers Branch and Carrollton. The recent Phase II Opening of the line represented the largest in DART's twenty-seven year history—surpassing even the debut of DART's light rail starter system in June 1996.

In addition to major employment destinations, the Green Line serves six internationally recognized medical centers, Dallas Market Center and Dallas Love Field Airport. It also connects commuters to five regional entertainment destinations, including Fair Park, Deep Ellum, the Dallas Arts District, the West End and Victory Park. This line is making it easier and faster for thousands of commuters to access work, shopping, medical, and educational and entertainment destinations across the region. In short, the Green Line changes everything!

Connections also continue to pop up along the Blue Line. The line now boasts a stop at Lake Highlands Station, which opened in December 2010. Nearby, the Lake Highlands Town Center, an ambitious, seventy acre, mixed-use, transit-oriented development is in the works. Meanwhile, construction continues on the 4.5 mile extension of the Blue Line from downtown Garland to Historic Downtown Rowlett. This $188 million project is scheduled for completion in December 2012. Construction also continues on the first part of the new Orange Line that will branch from the Green Line in northwest Dallas to serve the city of Irving. Altogether, the Green, Orange and Blue line expansion projects are expected to add 60,000 weekday passenger trips, nearly doubling ridership on the DART Rail System.

DART also continues to add to its award-winning history. The Texas Transit Association named DART its 2010 Outstanding Metropolitan Transit System and the Texas Department of Transportation honored President/Executive Director Gary Thomas with its 2010 Friend of Texas Transit Award for his overall management of the agency and his oversight of the Green Line project.

In addition, the Deep Ellum Gateway Project—a stainless steel sculpture series unveiled with the 2009 Phase I Green Line opening—has been honored by Americans for the Arts as one of the forty best public art installations in the country. Fair Park Station also made the list for its masterful take on the fairgrounds' unmatched collection of Art Deco exposition architecture.

Ready to get on board DART buses and trains? To get started, call DART Customer Information at 214-979-1111 with your origin, destination and desired time of travel. Helpful operators will recommend the most convenient route and departure time, quote the one-way fare, and advise you of any necessary transfers along the way. You can also plan trips online at www.DART.org.

When traveling in downtown Dallas, visit the DART Store at Akard Station for printed schedules or a system map. Schedules are also available at many libraries and other government centers in the DART Service Area.

If riding a DART bus or train does not fit your schedule, you can still save time and money by taking advantage of carpool or vanpool programs. DART's free RideShare computerized match list puts you in touch with other commuters with similar schedules and travel habits who want to share the ride.

For the latest DART news and information, visit www.DART.org. This information is also available in Spanish at www.transporteDART.org. If you have a web-enabled cell phone or PDA, visit the mobile website, m.dart.org, for on-the-go access to next scheduled bus and train information, point-to-point schedules and rider alerts.

See you on board!

Baylor Regional Medical Center at Plano

Backed by 100 years of experience, the Baylor Health Care System expanded into Collin County in December 2004 as it opened Baylor Regional Medical Center at Plano. Baylor Plano is an award-winning 112-bed hospital dedicated to serving families. Since opening, Baylor Plano has added new services and building space to help meet the specific health needs of adults in North Texas.

The center's extensive expansion now includes a seven story facility, which allowed the Center to grow from a ninety-six inpatient bed facility to a 112 bed facility in 2009. In January 2007, Baylor Plano became home to THE HEART HOSPITAL Baylor Plano, the first and only freestanding, full service hospital in this region dedicated solely to heart and vascular healthcare. A dedicated oncology unit and infusion and dialysis unit was added to Baylor Plano in June 2007. In 2008, Baylor Plano began construction on a second medical office pavilion. Among the many services that have been added to Baylor Plano since its opening are treatment for scoliosis and advanced spinal deformities at the Baylor Scoliosis Center, minimally invasive treatment for urological, gynecological and colo-rectal conditions through the daVinci® S Surgical System, and treatment for Barrett's Esophagus, a complication of GERD, or acid reflux, which if left untreated can become cancerous.

At Baylor Plano patients receive personalized attention from caregivers and benefit from healing in their own, private room. All larger than average, private rooms have oversized windows to provide generous light, thirty inch LCD television, and a free visitor wireless Internet network is available throughout the hospital. Additional hospital amenities include concierge service, family dining lounges with kitchenettes, room service offered from 7 am to 7 pm, business centers with computer access, free parking garage and valet service, pet therapy, full time pastoral care services for many faiths, garden level patio, free notary service to patients, and a smoke free campus.

Baylor Regional Medical Center at Plano has received numerous awards and recognition for providing quality service to North Texas communities, including being named a 2010 recipient of the Texas Award for Performance Excellence and has been designated by Blue Cross and Blue Shield of Texas, a Division of Health Care Service Corporation, as a Blue Distinction Center for Spine Surgery℠, a Blue Distinction Center for Knee and Hip Replacement℠ and a Blue Distinction Center for Bariatric Surgery®. The Baylor Plano Weight Loss Surgery Program was designated as a Center of Excellence by the American Society for Metabolic and Bariatric Surgery in January of 2008. Each year Collin College honors individuals and institutions for outstanding representation of Collin College's values and contributions to its mission, and in November of 2009, Baylor Plano was named a Living Legend for the hospital's unfaltering dedication to healing the body and strengthening the mind. In addition, Baylor Plano received The Pathway to Excellence™ designation of American Nurses Credentialing Center in September of 2007.

For more information regarding the outstanding services provided by Baylor Regional Medical Center, visit them online at www.BaylorHealth.com/Plano.

Note: Designation as Blue Distinction Centers® means these facilities' overall experience and aggregate data met objective criteria established in collaboration with expert clinicians' and leading professional organizations' recommendations. Individual outcomes may vary. To find out which services are covered under your policy at any facilities, please call your local Blue Cross and/or Blue Shield Plan.

Collin County Farm Bureau

Chartered on February 27, 1950, in McKinney, Texas, and regarded as the "Voice of Texas Agriculture," the Collin County Farm Bureau has successfully advanced the public policy interests of local farmers and ranchers for over a half century. Members benefit from the Bureau's wealth of personalized service in the areas of agricultural commodity marketing, discounts on consumer products and services, financial services through Farm Bureau Bank, vehicle rebates and insurance services offered by the Texas Farm Bureau Insurance Companies.

Regarded today as the largest Farm Bureau membership county in Texas with 11,894 members, the organization was first formed with less than 100 members as local farm and ranch families joined together to help solve their common problems through united action.

The Bureau's first elected Board of Directors included R. J. Wilson, Millard Rice, Tom West, R. L. Bellows, Murrell Rogers, L. R. Murrow, J. C. Loughlin, H. A. Kinney, Dwight Crigger, Carson Dillard, and Ruby Boren.

Over the past sixty years, the directors and officers of Collin County Farm Bureau have been some of the most prominent farmers and ranchers representing most every local community. Early leaders include: Millard Rice, John Wells, Tom West, Carson Dillard, John D. Truelove, W. C. Grissom, Harold Frazier, Edward Powell, Jack Miller, Gerald Furr and Robert Reynolds.

There have been three Collin County directors elected to serve on the Texas Farm Bureau state Board of Directors. These include the late Joe Fisher from McKinney, and Billie Ray Huddleston and Charles Ray Huddleston from Celina. Billie Ray was selected by the Texas board in 1990 to represent the organization as secretary/treasurer for three years and vice president for one year. Charles Ray is currently serving on the state board.

The current directors of the Bureau include Billie Ray Huddleston, John T. Rasor, Ben Scholz, Paul Furr, David McMahan, R. E. (Butch) Aycock, Jr., Dale Spurgin, Allan Littrell, Scott Bourland, Paul Lawrence, Randall Brockman, and Charles Ray Huddleston.

Throughout the years many member benefits have been added. Doyle Odom started the insurance services in 1950. Doyle and his wife Mamye worked together until Doyle passed away in 1978. Mamye continued to work in the agency until her retirement in 1991.

Dwain Gray has managed the insurance services since 1978. Office locations include McKinney, Farmersville, Plano, Frisco, Celina, Anna and Allen. For sixty years there have been only two managers and four county secretaries (Mary Margaret Dement, Mamye Odom, Pat Griffin and Carolyn McGarth). With positive board leadership and great stability the insurance services have grown to the current twenty-nine agents and fourteen staff members serving our members.

Actively involved in the life of the communities in which they serve, Collin County Farm Bureau has goals for the future including: continue to serve our membership effectively; work towards achieving an economic climate that will improve net farm income; educate the public regarding agricultural issues; promote free and fair trade; and protecting the interest of farmers and ranchers in Austin and Washington D.C.

Above: An August 1978 photograph commemorates the Open House celebration of 2,400 square feet of office space at 4009 West University Drive.

Below: In August 2010, the group celebrated the expansion of their offices to 9,060 square feet.

City of Richardson

First inhabited by the Comanche and Caddo Indian tribes who hunted the plentiful supply of deer and buffalo, the area that would one day be christened Richardson, Texas, began to draw young settlers and their families to its lush grass prairies in the 1840s.

Following the Civil War the railroad entered the area and brought a new and exciting future to lands across the South. Settlers rallied around the young community when William J. Wheeler donated land for the town site and railroad right-of-way. The city was named for railroad contractor E. H. Richardson, who built the rail line from Dallas to Denison.

In 1873, Richardson was chartered and many settlers from the nearby town of Breckinridge began to relocate to be closer to the new town. It included just three businesses—a general store, a post office and a drug store.

By the turn of the century, many Richardson residents were taking the train to Dallas to work. In 1908 the Interurban electric railway began service. By 1910 residents had seen their first telephone, electric light and gravel street and had grown in number to about 600. In 1914 the first schoolhouse, presently home to the administrative offices of the Richardson Independent School District (RISD), was built.

In 1924 the Red Brick Road (Greenville Avenue) was completed, bringing an increase in traffic and property values. The following year, the town was incorporated and elected its first mayor, Thomas F. McKamy. By that time, a total of fifteen businesses were in operation.

In 1926 waterworks and a sewage treatment plant were completed, the volunteer fire department was founded and utility franchises were awarded to Lone Star Gas and Texas Power and Light Company.

By 1950 the population stood at about 1,300 and the city was able to offer services such as an emergency ambulance, police protection and parks and recreation facilities.

Many transformative events would color the remainder of the twentieth century in and around Richardson. In 1951, Collins Radio opened a Richardson office and ushered the city into the electronic era.

Central Expressway opened in 1954 and the agricultural city of the past became a community of shopping centers and homes. In 1955, Richardson's first Police Department was organized and staffed by a police chief and two officers. Texas Instruments also opened its offices just south of the Richardson border and land values increased dramatically as the city made significant advances in population and economic status.

The city's population nearly tripled in the 1960s, from approximately 17,000 to about 49,000. This decade also saw a notable increase in the construction of landmark public facilities such as Huffhines Park, Prairie Creek Park and Cottonwood Park. The Southwest Center for Advanced Studies debuted in 1964 and became the University of Texas at Dallas in 1969.

Residential growth boomed through the 1970s and the city's commercial development continued to increase in the 1980s. In 1989, major expansion announcements by Richardson's MCI, Northern Telecom and Fujitsu, all telecommunications firms, led officials to dub Richardson the "Telecom Corridor®" of the Southwest and earned Richardson recognition from the *Wall Street Journal* as a suburban boomtown of the 1990s. During this same decade, there was a resurgence in residential development, which had slowed considerably in the economic downturn of the mid-1980s.

In the early 2000s, large investments were made at the University of Texas at Dallas to further semiconductor and bio-technological programs and to improve the image of the campus. The investments strengthened the city's role as a center for high-tech research and development. In 2009, Texas Instruments, Inc., started production at its wafer fabrication facility in the northern part of the city, one of the few analog microchip manufacturing operations in North America. The construction of a billion dollar data center project also began on the former Collins Radio corporate campus, and Blue Cross Blue Shield of Texas relocated its headquarters to a new location in the city.

Today, Richardson, Texas, is a thriving community with a population of more than 100,000 that boasts significant employment centers, retail areas and active, well-established corridors of high-tech research development that continue to blossom today.

Centennial Medical Center

We care completely at Centennial Medical Center, where your family's total wellbeing is our reason for being. Located off Highway 121 and Coit Road in Frisco, this full-service hospital offers an array of services ranging from maternity, radiology and pediatrics to sophisticated services such as neurosurgery, open heart surgery, and the latest procedures in joint replacement. We also have a twelve bed intensive care unit to care for the most critical patients.

The emergency department is fully accredited by the Society of Chest Pain Centers because of Centennial's commitment to high standards and quality of care that helps ensure our patients are neither sent home too early nor needlessly admitted during a coronary event. It is staffed with board-certified ER physicians, and their wait times are half the national average! You can see for yourself on our website www.CentennialMedCenter.com.

Centennial has all-inclusive maternity services that include a variety of classes, tours and support to help you prepare for what to expect when you are expecting. We have private LDR suites, mom/baby rooming, care packages, as well as a Level III Neonatal Intensive Care Unit to ensure the best possible care in any circumstance.

Centennial provides both nonsurgical and surgical options to help investigate, diagnose and treat neurological disorders and trauma. Whether you suffer from head injury, spinal problem, stroke or seizure, our comprehensive care team of neurologists, neurosurgeons, skilled nurses and physical therapists will help put your nervous system at ease.

In a cardiovascular emergency, time is of the essence. Be it a stroke or heart attack, you can take comfort in knowing the cardio center at Centennial is near and dear. It includes two interventional labs, an open-heart surgical program, and a host of cardiac diagnostic tools.

Whether suffering from pain caused by injury, illness, or nagging joint problems, it is comforting to know the orthopedic program at Centennial is here for you from diagnosis through recovery. Everyone from professional athletes in need of arthroscopic surgery to patients seeking relief from arthritis come to us to take a stand against join pain.

The Diabetes Program at Centennial Medical Center has been recognized by American Diabetes Association for our diabetes self-management education to people with diabetes, their families and loved ones.

Centennial's inpatient and outpatient Diagnostic Imaging Center employs digital technology to provide comfort, speed, accuracy and safety for all patients. Services include MRI, Ultrasound, Nuclear Medicine, 16- and 64-slice CT, stress testing, PET scan and interventional radiology.

Absolute care from absolute caregivers. It is why Centennial takes tremendous pride in delivering the utmost compassion and care to all who enter our doors.

Located at Highway 121 and Coit Road, Centennial Medical Center is Frisco's only full-service hospital.

Frisco RoughRiders

The era of professional baseball in North Texas began on April 3, 2003, as the Frisco RoughRiders played their inaugural home opener at Dr Pepper Ballpark in front of a sellout crowd of over 10,000 fans. The 'Riders won a prestigious off-the-field award in the first year of the franchise when named "Best New Ballpark for 2003" by baseballparks.com for its combination of superior design, attractive site selection, and fan amenities. The year 2003 also saw the 'Riders record a franchise record sixty-eight sellouts.

Since 2003 the RoughRiders have been a standard for minor league baseball excellence both on the field and off. The following season saw the 'Riders claim their first ever Texas League Championship. The club also led all of Double-A baseball in attendance—a feat they have accomplished in six consecutive seasons.

In 2005, Dr Pepper Ballpark hosted the Sixty-Ninth Texas League All-Star Game while the RoughRiders were awarded Texas League Team of the Year. The 'Riders front office was honored the next season when the club was awarded "Texas League Organization of the Year"—an award given to the RoughRiders again in 2010.

As the 'Riders continued improving both on the field and off, the front office received its highest award to date in 2007 when winning "The Bob Freitas Award for Organization of the Year." Given annually to the top minor league franchise in the nation for front office excellence, the Freitas award is among the most coveted in the industry.

While the industry leaders recognized the club's front office, the fans were more focused on the club's two best ambassadors: mascots Deuce and Daisy. These two zany prairie dogs entertain the Frisco faithful with their in-between inning antics involving fans, umpires, and even the players. With over 100 different skits, Deuce and Daisy give fans plenty of reasons to come out to the ballpark.

The RoughRiders continue to provide North Texans one of the most unique, affordable, and fun forms of entertainment in the entire region. As the Double-A affiliate of the Texas Rangers, baseball fans have the opportunity to watch and interact with future major league stars before they become household names. In fact, in 2010, three of the five Rangers selected to the major league All-Star game were former RoughRiders (Elvis Andrus, Ian Kinsler, and Neftali Feliz).

The Frisco RoughRiders have had success on the field and in the front office and have seen over 4.7 million fans pour through the turnstiles at Dr Pepper Ballpark. Many leave with a souvenir or an autograph, but all leave with a smile!

✧

Photographs courtesy of James Garner.

Texas Health Presbyterian Hospital Plano

Since opening in 1991, Texas Health Presbyterian Hospital Plano (THP) has become an integral part of a rapidly growing community and now prepares to celebrate its twentieth anniversary of caring for the communities it serves. The hospital's staff has grown, its technology has expanded, but the commitment to providing comfort and care to those seeking quality health services remains.

THP is among thirteen member hospitals that make up Texas Health Resources (THR) and today includes a 366-bed critical care facility offering a full range of medical specialties, including back and spine, critical care services, heart and vascular, highly specialized neonatal care, oncology, orthopedics, pediatrics, and women's health services. THP employs over 1,600 people, has a medical staff of over 1,300 physicians, and cares for over 16,000 inpatients and 110,000 outpatients annually.

Philip M. Wentworth, FACHE, retired as president of THP in March 2009. Dedicated to the visionary care of the organization and the communities it served, he created a great legacy of clinical and service excellence. Wentworth had been with Presbyterian Healthcare System for thirty years, sixteen of which were with THP. During his years at THP, the hospital grew enormously under his guidance and received numerous recognitions and awards.

Jim Boswell was another instrumental leader for the hospital. As an Administrative Director for THP, he made many contributions during his fifteen-year tenure. Under his leadership, he helped with recruitment of physicians and development of a strong physician relations program, as well as community relations initiatives. He served the hospital tirelessly until his death in May 2010.

THP has been the recipient of several prestigious awards including the Texas Award for Performance Excellence in 2008. The award's criteria are based on consistent performance at high levels of quality. THP was the first healthcare facility in Collin County and only the fourth in Texas to receive this honor. The hospital has also received the coveted Magnet Recognition Program® Award for excellence in nursing services, which remains one of the country's most prestigious designations honoring nursing quality. Additional accolades include Level III Trauma Designation, Bariatric Center of Excellence, and Chest Pain Accreditation.

THP has also received the Ivy Award, a national restaurant industry accolade given to a select group of restaurants, hotels, and noncommercial food operators that exemplify the highest standards of excellence in food and service. Texas Health Plano received the award by *Restaurants and Institutions* magazine, which hailed the hospital's Five-Star Dining Program for patients, employees, and guests.

For more information about Texas Health Plano, please call 1-877-THR-WELL or visit www.texashealth.org.

AG-POWER, INC.

Above: With the growth of the Ag-Power organization, it became necessary to obtain additional space for the administrative aspects of the business, so the Administrative and Accounting Departments moved to space in the current Independent Bank building on Redbud Boulevard. Construction of a new facility began in 2009 that would house the dealership and the administration/ account departments. In April 2010 the new facility at 3501 North Central Expressway opened as a state-of-the-art John Deere Place with over 66,000 square feet, which includes 18,000 in display and sales, 13,000 in parts, 24,000 in service bays and 11,000 in administrative offices.

Below: Jack and Kym Radke, owners of Ag-Power, Inc.

Originally founded by the Settle family of Prosper in 1972, Ag-Power is a full-line John Deere Dealership providing sales, parts and service of agricultural, lawn and garden and commercial products. Recently, the company has included the Honda & Stihl lines to compliment the John Deere line. Once, primarily selling mostly large agricultural equipment to the farmers in Collin County, Ag-Power has adjusted to the changing needs of its customers by offering smaller ag equipment as well as lawn and commercial equipment to meet the changing needs in Collin County.

Full aftermarket service is an integral part of the business. Offering a well-stocked parts inventory (John Deere and competitive parts), customers can get the parts they need for whatever equipment they own and if not in stock, most parts can be obtained overnight. A well-trained service staff is available to assist the customer in keeping their equipment running with as little down-town as possible, while a large fleet of Service Field trucks also assists by servicing equipment, whether it is large ag equipment or lawn mowers, at the customer's location. The trucks are also equipped with laptop computers to help diagnose problems.

As large cotton, grain and dairy farmers, the Settle family learned to rely on Mother Nature to produce their crops, but also realized the importance of good, dependable farm equipment. The family became a John Deere dealer and opened Settle Machinery Company in 1972 in a small Quonset building located on Highway 289 (now Preston Road) in Frisco. They moved the dealership to McKinney in 1973 to a new facility located on Highway 380, four miles west of Central Expressway and expanded and remodeled the business in 1993.

In 1988, Jack Radke, a former John Deere employee, bought into the business and it became Settle-Radke Machinery. Prior to this acquisition, Jack had been employed with John Deere Company for twelve years with various assignments throughout the Deere organization.

When Jack and Ronnie Settle were partners, as well as after the organization became Ag-Power, the business grew from a one store operation to eleven dealer locations throughout north and northeast Texas. In 2005, Jack bought Ronnie's share of the business and became the sole owner of Ag-Power, Inc.

Today, Ag-Power is one of the largest volume John Deere dealer organizations in the nation and includes approximately 200 employees at locations in Terrell, Mineola, Paris, Sulphur Springs, Sherman, Mount Pleasant, Tyler, Rhome and Athens. In January of 2011 the eleventh location in Fort Worth was added as a pilot program along with John Deere Landscapes.

Ag-Power and its locations participate in many of their local events and county fairs by providing equipment and manpower. Annually, the organization participates as a major sponsor in the State Fair of Texas and the Fort Worth Stock Show and Rodeo, and supports the Relay for Life and Susan G. Komen races by providing equipment for local events.

For more information, visit the company online at www.ag-power.com.

Bob Tomes Ford

The Bob and Barbara Tomes story began in McKinney in 1983, when the couple opened Bob Tomes Ford with 17 employees and 20 vehicles.

Bob graduated from the University of Nebraska and went on to enlist in the U.S. Army in 1968. An Officer Candidate School graduate, Bob was assigned to the Military Assistance Command in the Mekong Delta of Vietnam and was awarded the Bronze Star for meritorious service. Bob returned to Nebraska and was hired by the Ford Motor Company in Omaha in 1972 followed by a promotion and transfer to Houston in 1977.

Barbara graduated from SMU, and went to work for the Ford Motor Company.

The couple met in a chance meeting in the shared mailroom between the sales and customer service divisions where their affection for one another grew. Thereafter, they were married.

Bob and Barbara began selling Ford vehicles in McKinney on January 17, 1983 on a 3.8 acre lot with about two dozen vehicles. In 1988 they moved their dealership to the five-acre site where it currently stands.

Bob Tomes Ford is a full service dealership and currently spans sixteen acres. They are Blue Oval Certified, winners of the President's Award for Customer Service Satisfaction and recognized in 2001 as the "Business of the Year" by the Chamber of Commerce.

The success of the Tomes dealership can be linked to their significant presence in the McKinney community.

Barbara served as a board member for the Boys and Girls Club of Collin County and as the president of the Heard-Craig Center. Her volunteerism includes having served on the task force for the city of McKinney's 150th birthday, involvement with the Boy Scouts and the First United Methodist Church. Barbara is on the board of the McKinney Education Foundation, the McKinney Alliance, and a local bank. Bob and Barbara were also selected as Chamber of Commerce "Volunteers of the Year" in 1991.

Bob and Barbara's contributions to education include: The McKinney Education Foundation, Bob Tomes Ford Endowment Fund Scholarship, and the National Future Farmers of America Scholarships.

Dedicated to the betterment and support of both his industry and community, Bob has volunteered for the McKinney United Way (past chairman), Volunteer McKinney Center, past chairman of the board of the McKinney Chamber of Commerce, McKinney Rotary Club past president, Paul Harris Society, and is a lifetime member of the American Legion. Bob is involved with the Boy Scouts and currently serves on the Texas Health Resources board (Presbyterian Hospital). Bob was also a five-year member of the board of directors for the McKinney Economic Development Corporation.

Professionally, Bob is a member of the National Automobile Dealer's Association and currently serves as a board member for Texas Automobile Dealer Association and North Texas Ford Dealer's Advertising Fund. Recognized by Ford Motor Company as a 2010 Salute to Dealers' Nominee, 2008 Ford Motor Credit Company Partner in Quality Award recipient, and one of sixty-six dealer nominees from across America for the 2002 *Time Magazine* Quality Dealer of the Year Award.

Bob and Barbara's son, Brandon, graduated from SMU and joined them in the business and became a minority partner in 2008. He graduated from the National Automobile Dealer's Association Dealer Candidate Academy in July 2009. In November 2010, Brandon opened Brandon Tomes Subaru.

"We're always looking through the front windshield and not the rear-view mirror," commented Bob. "It feels good to make improvements based on our participation."

"McKinney means a lot to us. This is our home."

Below: The Tomes family.

Bottom: Bob Tomes Ford, 950 South Central Expressway, McKinney, Texas, 214-544-5000.

North Texas History Center

Located in McKinney, Texas, the county seat of Collin County, The North Texas History Center is a multi-purpose facility dedicated to serving the larger community—local, regional and national. Founded in 1957 as the Collin County Historical Society, NTHC has grown with the community around it. As of this writing Collin County is nationally known as one of the fastest growing and most affluent communities in the United States.

Long a repository of genealogical research resources, in 1982 the Collin County Historical Society opened the door to its museum, housed in an early twentieth century building that once served as the post office for McKinney, Texas. In 2005 the historical society was awarded the prestigious Museums for America Grant which provided for the physical inventory of its collections. Subsequent grants helped establish interpretive exhibits that attracted local citizens and those throughout the Northeast Texas region.

The Collin County Historical Society became the North Texas History Center in 2007 and began to acquire archival materials from other institutions. In 2008 the NTHC acquired the genealogical collection of Denton County; in so doing it became the repository for primary source material on many historic figures associated with the early cattle industry in Texas, like John Simpson Chisum, his relatives and family. This enhances our existing information about the industry that first brought wealth to Texas after the Civil War. The Sedalia or Shawnee Trail, the first of the major cattle trails from Texas to markets in the Northern United States, came through Collin County, where many of the early "Cattle Kings" were residents. These and many other historical figures are represented in the Center's extensive collection of 60,000 historic photographs.

Traditional western history resources are not the only subject matter offered to the public. Museum personnel have conducted many community events, cultural expositions and exhibits. The NTHC also works in partnership with various historical preservation groups in the identification of significant landmarks. In the future the center has plans to serve as an archaeological processing and cataloging facility working in conjunction with educational institutions. Also in the center's future will be the participation in project-based consortiums dedicated to preserving the history of Northeast Texas.

Our vision celebrates, values, and supports interpretation of history of place, person and traditions with a broad and multi-faceted perspective. Our mission is to serve by preserving, collecting and exhibiting our cultural resources to nurture the understanding of the diverse human experience that is unique to North Texas.

Sponsors

For more information about the following publications or about publishing your own book, please call Historical Publishing Network at 800-749-9790 or visit www.lammertinc.com.

Albemarle & Charlottesville: An Illustrated History of the First 150 Years
Black Gold: The Story of Texas Oil & Gas
Garland: A Contemporary History
Historic Abilene: An Illustrated History
Historic Alamance County: An Illustrated History
Historic Albuquerque: An Illustrated History
Historic Alexandria: An Illustrated History
Historic Amarillo: An Illustrated History
Historic Anchorage: An Illustrated History
Historic Austin: An Illustrated History
Historic Baldwin County: A Bicentennial History
Historic Baton Rouge: An Illustrated History
Historic Beaufort County: An Illustrated History
Historic Beaumont: An Illustrated History
Historic Bexar County: An Illustrated History
Historic Birmingham: An Illustrated History
Historic Brazoria County: An Illustrated History
Historic Brownsville: An Illustrated History
Historic Charlotte: An Illustrated History of Charlotte and Mecklenburg County
Historic Chautauqua County: An Illustrated History
Historic Cheyenne: A History of the Magic City
Historic Clayton County: An Illustrated History
Historic Comal County: An Illustrated History
Historic Corpus Christi: An Illustrated History
Historic DeKalb County: An Illustrated History
Historic Denton County: An Illustrated History
Historic Edmond: An Illustrated History
Historic El Paso: An Illustrated History
Historic Erie County: An Illustrated History
Historic Fayette County: An Illustrated History
Historic Fairbanks: An Illustrated History
Historic Gainesville & Hall County: An Illustrated History
Historic Gregg County: An Illustrated History
Historic Hampton Roads: Where America Began
Historic Hancock County: An Illustrated History
Historic Henry County: An Illustrated History
Historic Hood County: An Illustrated History
Historic Houston: An Illustrated History
Historic Hunt County: An Illustrated History
Historic Illinois: An Illustrated History
Historic Kern County: An Illustrated History of Bakersfield and Kern County
Historic Lafayette: An Illustrated History of Lafayette & Lafayette Parish
Historic Laredo: An Illustrated History of Laredo & Webb County
Historic Lee County: The Story of Fort Myers & Lee County
Historic Louisiana: An Illustrated History
Historic Mansfield: A Bicentennial History
Historic Midland: An Illustrated History
Historic Mobile: An Illustrated History of the Mobile Bay Region
Historic Montgomery County: An Illustrated History of Montgomery County, Texas
Historic Ocala: The Story of Ocala & Marion County
Historic Oklahoma: An Illustrated History
Historic Oklahoma County: An Illustrated History
Historic Omaha: An Illustrated History of Omaha and Douglas County
Historic Orange County: An Illustrated History
Historic Osceola County: An Illustrated History
Historic Ouachita Parish: An Illustrated History
Historic Paris and Lamar County: An Illustrated History
Historic Pasadena: An Illustrated History
Historic Passaic County: An Illustrated History
Historic Pennsylvania An Illustrated History
Historic Philadelphia: An Illustrated History
Historic Prescott: An Illustrated History of Prescott & Yavapai County
Historic Richardson: An Illustrated History
Historic Rio Grande Valley: An Illustrated History
Historic Rogers County: An Illustrated History
Historic San Marcos: An Illustrated History
Historic Santa Barbara: An Illustrated History
Historic Scottsdale: A Life from the Land
Historic Shelby County: An Illustrated History
Historic Shreveport-Bossier: An Illustrated History of Shreveport & Bossier City
Historic South Carolina: An Illustrated History
Historic Smith County: An Illustrated History
Historic Temple: An Illustrated History
Historic Texarkana: An Illustrated History
Historic Texas: An Illustrated History
Historic Victoria: An Illustrated History
Historic Tulsa: An Illustrated History
Historic Wake County: An Illustrated History
Historic Warren County: An Illustrated History
Historic Williamson County: An Illustrated History
Historic Wilmington & The Lower Cape Fear: An Illustrated History
Historic York County: An Illustrated History
Iron, Wood & Water: An Illustrated History of Lake Oswego
Jefferson Parish: Rich Heritage, Promising Future
Miami's Historic Neighborhoods: A History of Community
Old Orange County Courthouse: A Centennial History
Plano: An Illustrated Chronicle
The New Frontier: A Contemporary History of Fort Worth & Tarrant County
Rich With Opportunity: Images of Beaumont and Jefferson County
San Antonio, City Exceptional
The San Gabriel Valley: A 21st Century Portrait
Southwest Louisiana: A Treasure Revealed
The Spirit of Collin County
Valley Places, Valley Faces
Water, Rails & Oil: Historic Mid & South Jefferson County